Frederick A. (Frederick Albion) Ober

The Knockabout Club in North Africa

Frederick A. (Frederick Albion) Ober

The Knockabout Club in North Africa

ISBN/EAN: 9783743308138

Manufactured in Europe, USA, Canada, Australia, Japa

Cover: Foto ©ninafisch / pixelio.de

Manufactured and distributed by brebook publishing software (www.brebook.com)

Frederick A. (Frederick Albion) Ober

The Knockabout Club in North Africa

THE MAMELUKE'S LEAP. — *Frontispiece.*

The
Knockabout Club

IN

North Africa

BY

FRED A. OBER

FULLY ILLUSTRATED

BOSTON
ESTES AND LAURIAT
PUBLISHERS

Copyright, 1890,
BY ESTES AND LAURIAT.

All Rights Reserved.

UNIVERSITY PRESS:
JOHN WILSON AND SON, CAMBRIDGE, U.S.A.

CONTENTS.

Chapter		Page
I.	A Peep into the Dark Continent from Gibraltar to Tangier	11
II.	Ten Days in Tangier. — Snake-charmers and Arab Dens	27
III.	A Caravan Journey to Fez. — The Powder-play, and the Sultan	47
IV.	Morocco and the Moors	63
V.	Some Time in a Pirate City	77
VI.	A Railroad Journey in Algiers	94
VII.	Arab Tombs and Arab Cities	111
VIII.	The "Diamond in an Emerald Setting"	134
IX.	In the Corsairs' Stronghold. — The Doctor tells an Indian Story	148
X.	All about the Algerians	167
XI.	A Lion-hunt in the Aures Mountains	183
XII.	Tunis, Carthage, and the Great Desert	195
XIII.	From Tripoli to Egypt	214
XIV.	The Pyramids and the Nile	229

ILLUSTRATIONS.

	PAGE
The Mameluke's Leap	Frontispiece
A Beggar of Tangier	12
On Board the Steamer	14
The Rock of Gibraltar	17
Moonlight on the Mediterranean	19
Nearing the Coast of Africa	20
A View of Tangier from the Sea	22
Tangier	23
Snake-charming	29
Jews of Tangier	33
The Grand Mosque, Tangier	36
The Morning Prayers	37
Arab Woman of Tangier	41
Principal Street of Tangier	45
Amusements on the Journey	48
The Powder-play	49
Interior of a Moorish Mosque	53
An Officer of the Moorish Legation	57
Feats of Horsemanship	59
Travelling in Morocco	61
A Solitary Tree on the Plain	64
A Scene in Morocco	65
On the Coast of Morocco	67
A Rapid Gait	69
A Moorish Festival	69
The City of Morocco	71
Arabian Travellers	73
A Soldier of Morocco	74
A Moorish Band of Music	75
Natives of Morocco	78
A Moor	79
Feats of Horsemanship at the Fête of Mahomet	80
Nemours	83
Fête at the Anniversary of the Birth of Mahomet	89
Tailpiece	93
Travelling in Algeria	96
Mosque of Sidi Abd-er-Rahhmann	98
An Algerian Beauty	99
An Algerian Antelope-hunter	103
Mosque of Sidi Salahh, at Ouargla	108
An Oasis of the Algerian Sahara	109
The Moorish Method of Ploughing	113
A Young Moor	115
A Moorish General	117
Musicians of Morocco	121
Tlemcen	125
At the End of a Journey	129
An Oasis in the Desert	136
Decatur's Fight with the Algerian	143
Stephen Decatur	146
An Equestrian Dance	153
Merchant and Camel	157
Door of Mosque of Bou Medina	161
Tailpiece	166
Arab Women of the Interior	169
Moorish Women at Home	173

ILLUSTRATIONS.

	PAGE		PAGE
A Bride being conducted to her Husband's Home	175	Mosque of Sidi Ben Ferdha, Biskra	201
The Arab's Song of Victory	177	The Native Quarter of Biskra	202
The Conceited Young Lion	179	Mosque of Sidi Mohhammed, at Biskra	203
"The lions began to arrive"	181	"A fearful roar thundered from the mountains"	209
A Lion and a Lioness	185	Repelling Arab Robbers	215
An Oasis appearing in a Mirage to Travellers in the Desert	189	The Citadel of Tripoli	216
A Mountain Pass in Tunis	191	Decatur Sailing into the Harbor of Tripoli	217
Medjerdab, the most important River in Tunis	193	A View of Tripoli	220
		Donkey-Boys	225
A Mosque in Tunis	194	Man's Willing Slave	230
A View of the New Portion of Biskra	196	Pyramids and Sphinx	231
Camping-place in Sight of Biskra	197	Egyptian Garden and Temple	235

THE KNOCKABOUT CLUB IN NORTH AFRICA.

" *Seated in a Moorish garden*
 On the Sahel of Algiers,
 Wandering breezes brought the burden
 Of its history in past years.
 Lost amid the mist of ages
 Its first chronicles arise;
 Yonder is the chain of Atlas
 And the Pagan paradise.

" *Past these shores the wise Phœnicians*
 Coasted onward toward the West,
 Hoping there to find Atlantis,
 And the Islands of the Blest.
 Somewhere in these mystic valleys
 Grew the golden-fruited trees
 Which the wandering sons of Zeus
 Stole from the Hesperides."

THE KNOCKABOUT CLUB IN NORTH AFRICA.

CHAPTER I.

A PEEP INTO THE DARK CONTINENT FROM GIBRALTAR TO TANGIER.

STANDING upon the topmost rock that capped the fortifications at Gibraltar, the Professor and I resolved to penetrate into the continent spread out before us. It was new to us, yet occupied by the oldest races of mankind. It lay before us invitingly, — this unexplored region, Africa, — its plains smiling in sunshine, its hills rising into mountains. Only a narrow strait separated us from the northern coast of the Dark Continent. A few hours' sail would take us to that land of mysteries, the home of the fierce Arab, of the camel, the lion, elephant, gorilla, giraffe.

It was not our intention to strive for Equatorial Africa, for the Mountains of the Moon, the Congo, or the sources of the Nile. We were not equipped for that; but we were quite prepared to go into Morocco, to essay a caravan trip across the Great Desert, to hunt the lion in the mountains of Aures, to tent with the Bedouin, and to explore the most attractive portion of Algeria. This, in brief, is our plan, and we cordially invite you to join us.

Perhaps some of our readers have already accompanied us on former expeditions, — waded with us through the Everglades, sailed the Antilles, or tramped with us through historic Spain. This being the case, you may share our feelings, and yearn for some new country to conquer. You are welcome to go with us, dear reader, even though we have never met you and may never see you. Join, then, the silent caravan of people we never see, of friends whose voices we never hear, yet whose presence we ever feel, inciting us to new endeavor and higher effort. Believe us, we would like to be of service to you; we would like to provide for you such entertainment and such instruction that it will be good for you that you have been with us. We may, doubtless, we do, seem dim and shadowy to you, because we hide our personality under assumed titles; but we are nevertheless alive, dear friends, and may move among you,

A BEGGAR OF TANGIER.

and have acquaintance with friends of yours. Our adventures are none the less real because they are not always given in the "first person singular." It may be our modesty, or pure affectation, that causes us to hide our identity; but you may rely upon the authenticity of our descriptions and the truthfulness of our natures. Only truth will prevail at the last, and he only shall stand who tells the truth.

As we have already stated in another "Knockabout," our motive for travel is found in the desire to learn, and especially to study the history of the various countries of the world. We like to see for ourselves the countries where great events have taken place, and meet the strange people of historic lands. The Professor has a somewhat scientific turn of mind, and is inclined to be rather absorbed in his work, and (between you and me) he is not always so companionable as he ought to be. Why, I have known him to spend half a day hunting for arrow-heads, or stone chisels, or some other relics of early Indians, and even neglect his meals on account of some strange bug or plant that he considered of more value than humanity. Now, of course the Professor has a great deal in him of value, if you can only get it out of him. That is what I am constantly doing, or trying to do, — forcing my companion to disgorge some of his valuable information; and then I try to put it in an entertaining shape. So if you find any dull or prosy things in this book you must set them down to the Professor; and if you find anything really good, why — modesty forbids that I mention the name that ought to have the credit. As for myself, the Historian, perhaps the less said the better. I am one half of the Siamese twin, as we may say, and the Professor is the other. Between us we hope to interest you, at all events.

Well, as I began, we took our first survey of the African coast from the Rock of Gibraltar, and then descended to take steamer for Tangier, the port of Morocco, at which we purposed beginning our African explorations. As we reached the quay, the steamer came to anchor in the harbor, and we hired a boatman to row us out. He was a villanous-looking fellow, the very worst type of a Rock Scorpion, as the Spanish natives of Gibraltar are called. As soon as we entered the boat, the Professor became interested in a species of sponge and a barnacle that lay in the bottom, and was so absorbed that he did not notice the wild looks of our boatman as we neared the steamer. The Rock Scorpion landed us, however, the sailors hoisted our baggage on board, and I put into his hand just double the amount he had agreed on as fare. That was a mistake, as I soon saw, for it

ON BOARD THE STEAMER.

excited the Scorpion's cupidity, and he demanded as much more. The feeling of compassion that had prompted me to double the fare changed at once to contempt at his meanness, and

I of course promptly refused. The Scorpion became furiously enraged, dashed his hat into the boat, tightened his leather belt about his waist, and swore that he would have double fare or throw me into the sea. I was then standing on the lower step of the ladder, the ship's side towering over me, and clinging by one hand. I looked up and around, and saw that I was at the mercy of the Scorpion, for there wasn't anybody else in sight. The Professor, having become interested in the sponge, had taken it on deck to examine, while the sailors, after having hoisted our luggage on board, had disappeared. But I was determined not to accede to the man's demands, for it was a matter of principle and not of money.

Seeing my almost defenceless position, the Scorpion made a pass at me with his hand, which I parried; and then he ran to the stern of the boat and drew out of the locker a long knife. I did not wait for his return, but scampered up the ladder as fast as my legs could carry me; yet he, being a sailor, and better used to the rolling of the ship, was half-way up the ladder before I could reach the gangway. I could hear his panting, could almost feel his hot breath on my back. Another minute and I should be safe on board, where I hoped some one would intercept him. But I slipped at the top step and came down upon my knees. That was almost fatal to me, for the Scorpion at once sprang on my back. I could feel his grip at my waistband; then I saw the long knife flash before my face.

It was little use to struggle, because the Scorpion had me at such disadvantage; yet I tried to raise myself and throw him off. Thinking, probably, that he had me at his mercy, he played with me as a cat plays with the mouse in her grasp, and for a few seconds delayed striking me. He seemed to have forgotten the cause of dispute, but was now so wild with passion that his only thought was to kill me. At such times men of this stamp do not allow reason to have a voice; they are insane, worse even than brutes. I had my wits at work, though, and as he dallied with the knife I half turned about and seized his arm. This quick motion probably saved my life, for it diverted his attention, and just at that moment relief came to me. A hand was thrust over my shoulder, and the man's throat was in its grasp. This enabled me to slip out from under him, seize the knife, and throw it overboard. At about the same time, or as soon as it was accomplished, a vigorous kick from the person who had come to my rescue sent the Scorpion spinning down the ladder and into the sea. He floundered about awhile, but soon clambered into his boat and sullenly rowed away. He was thoroughly cowed; he had played a desperate game and had lost.

Looking up to thank my deliverer, I was astonished to see a familiar face.

"Why, Doctor, is it you?"

"The same," answered a cheery voice; "nobody else than yours truly."

I silently pressed his hand, and he knew that my gratitude was greater than I could express in words.

"All right, old fellow; don't mention it. Glad I came in the nick of time. Think the Scorp meant to stick you. That was an ugly-looking knife he had. But I just enjoyed kicking him down the ladder. It isn't often I have a chance to get even with the beggars. So you don't owe me anything; the act was its own reward."

"But, Doctor, where did you come from? How came you here?"

"Oh, a short story soon told. Been in France over a year. Met a man you knew in Spain; said you were going to Africa; so took steamer at Marseilles and headed you off."

"Good! and you will go with us?"

"Go? Of course I'll go. What else did I come here for?

THE ROCK OF GIBRALTAR.

Can't let two babes like you and Professor wander off into the wilds alone. Made plenty money in Paris; have come down here to spend it. I'll head the caravan, with your permission, and will go along, any way. Where is the Professor? Mooning about over some old relic, as usual, of course."

We soon found the Professor, who seemed very glad to have the Doctor join us, remarking that now we should have somebody at the head of affairs who would make those Arabs mind their business.

MOONLIGHT ON THE MEDITERRANEAN.

The Doctor, by the way, had been our companion in the Antilles, and had amused us with his sprightly ways and kept up our spirits with his never-failing good-humor. I especially welcomed the Doctor, since the Professor was always so wrapped up in himself that he was hardly aware of my presence. As we sat on the hurricane deck the Doctor questioned us as to our plans.

"Now, in the first place," he said, "Africa is a big country; as a continent, it ranks with the three largest divisions of the globe. It is nearly five thousand miles long, and forty-six hundred wide in its broadest part, extending over seventy-two degrees of latitude, — from latitude 37° north of the equator to 35° south, — and between Greenwich longitude 52° east and 18° west. We are told that it is about twelve million miles in area, and has a population of perhaps one hundred million. Now, what I want to know is, what part of this big continent you intend to explore. If it's part of it I'm with you; if it's the whole of it I am still there, even if you tramp all over its twelve million miles of area." This was a remarkably long and connected speech for the Doctor, and he paused to take breath, while the Professor cleared his throat preparatory to enlightening him.

NEARING THE COAST OF AFRICA.

"My dear boy," said the Professor, in a fatherly way, "you always remind me of a gun, — an old muzzle-loader, single-barrel gun, — for when you are once loaded and are touched off, you discharge your entire load, and are then as empty as ever! Now that you have given us all the geographical and statistical information you possess, — for which we are truly grateful, though we knew it all before, — we will proceed to fill you up with new material, that you may not remain entirely empty. Know, then, that we do not propose to accomplish the exploration of all Africa in a single year. Other men, far greater than we, have spent their lives in exploring a comparatively small portion of this Dark Continent. We shall not even go into Equatorial Africa, and shall certainly leave the Congo and the sources of the Nile to the intrepid Stanley. We want to acquaint ourselves with that portion lying between the Straits of Gibraltar and Tunis, because we know that is all we can properly investigate in the time at our disposal. Our main object is to study the Arabs and native peoples in their homes, and become acquainted with an Oriental civilization. We are going to begin with Morocco, and shall first land at Tangier, and provide ourselves with guides and escort for the interior, where I expect our most exciting adventures will begin."

"And there it is now," said the Doctor, rising from his seat.

Behind us, dim in distance, lay Gibraltar, before us Tangier, chief port of Morocco.

Gibraltar, we have already described. We left it the same day we arrived. Arriving at six in the morning, the steamer for Tangier departed at eleven that forenoon. Great cloud-masses hung over Spain, beneath them the burnished shields of the Sierra Nevadas, while the African coast lay before us clear and green and smiling. And in the afternoon Tangier lay before us, the ancient *Tandja*, "city protected by the Lord," the oldest city, perhaps, of this part of Africa. It lies on a slope, not unlike Algiers, its white walls sparkling in the sun, though it has no protected harbor like Algiers, and it is a long distance from the steamer anchorage to the mole. Crowning the triangular town is the *Kasba*, the citadel; batteries flank it and frown along the shore; a dome here and there breaks the outline, and three minarets rise above the sea of roofs. The Bay of Tangier is magnificent in its breadth and sweep, but it is shallow. A yellow beach curves around in front of a pleasing landscape of fields and low hills, and one hill in particular is green with gardens on its slopes.

A noisy swarm of Arabs surrounded the steamer at once, and to their untried mercies we were intrusted. There was no help for it, so into the boats we went, our luggage tumbling after, and away our wild boatmen rowed, singing, shouting, and swearing, for the yellow beach. But they were not so very bad to us, and charged us but two francs each for the voyage, including the luggage. The latter they landed on the beach, and then brought us before the officers of the customs. This was an ordeal we had long dreaded,

A VIEW OF TANGIER FROM THE SEA.

for people of our own blood had often treated us barbarously at the customs, and what could we expect from piratical Mahometans? There was no custom-house, but in lieu thereof an old dry-goods box, upon which sat a grave and dignified Turk; at least, he looked like a Turk, and doubtless was. He was wrapped in an ample robe of white, had an immense turban on his head, and a long white beard flowed down to his girdle. He looked like a patriarch, not even Abraham himself more so. He fixed his eye on us, but said no word. I trembled as my trunk was brought before him, and did not doubt that the next minute I should be ordered to the bastinado. He

TANGIER.

waved his hand; an obedient servant opened the trunk; he waved his hand again, and the servant closed it. That was all. Not a word had been said, but I was free to enter Tangier. Immediately a hungry horde of Arabs pounced upon me. They seized me and my trunk and valises, and pulled me and them in every direction at once. They led me and my fellow-sufferers through numerous winding ways till we came to the Hotel Continental, said to be the best in the place, but only to find it full. Even the bath-tub had an occupant, the French proprietor told us.

Then we were saved as by a miracle. Early in the fray I had been pounced upon by a stalwart Arab, who drove away all the smaller ones, appropriated all my luggage, which he carried easily upon his brawny shoulders, and took me under his special charge.

"Come with me," he said, in Spanish. "I will take the Señor to a hotel where the charges are cheap and the fare is good, though few people go there, because it is kept by a Spaniard."

Then he led us through other narrow streets and winding lanes, until we brought up at the Fonda Iberica, kept by Nicholas Fernandez. It was in an obscure quarter of the city, so surrounded by Arab dens and houses that we could never find it without a guide; but it was kept as well as the worthy Don Nicholas could afford, the host and hostess were kindly, and it was the only hotel not full of strangers. This Fonda Iberica, — the Iberian Hotel, — to which the Spaniard had given the ancient name of Spain itself, Iberus, was, as I have said, in a street so narrow and obscure that I could only approximately locate it by remembering that there was a *fuente*, a fountain, in the market-place, somewhere near the spot where the street turned off and began its devious windings and tunnellings.

My guide was called Mahomet, though this name did not distinguish him, for every other man and boy in Tangier bears the same cognomen. He was an Arab, and wore the customary costume, —

the *gehab* or the *burnous*, a flowing robe without sleeves, of cotton, adorned with a *capote*, like a monk's hood, which reached from neck to heels; a greasy fez, once red, on his head, the tassel jauntily dangling; on his bare feet red slippers, with their heels chopped off, his heels hanging over the soles, cracked and grimy with dirt at least a quarter of an inch thick. Mahomet had a swinging gait, and a rollicking, swash-buckler air, that bore out his statement that he had served years in the royal guard. He by right of discovery claimed me as his exclusive property, and resented any assumption of right in any one else. During my stay in Tangier he clung to me tenaciously, and went with me everywhere.

I find in my note-book this comment, written at the beginning of our acquaintance: "I think he is a rascal, but he probably has his price, and the only question between us, I apprehend, will be the difference betwixt his price and mine." To his credit let me say it, he did not prove extortionate.

After I had rested, Mahomet conducted me to and through the market-place in the outskirts of the city, called the *Sok*. We passed first through the city square, a paved place surrounded with shops, and, like all the streets, filthy in the extreme, with piles of garbage, pools of slime and mud, stacks of dead cats, rats, fowls, and ordure. Through these Stygian pools the Arabs paddled serenely in their white robes, scarcely noticing any obstruction, whether of filth, foreigner, or donkey.

CHAPTER II.

TEN DAYS IN TANGIER. — SNAKE-CHARMERS AND ARAB DENS.

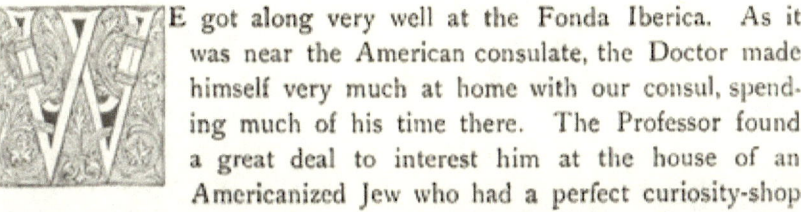E got along very well at the Fonda Iberica. As it was near the American consulate, the Doctor made himself very much at home with our consul, spending much of his time there. The Professor found a great deal to interest him at the house of an Americanized Jew who had a perfect curiosity-shop of Oriental things; and many a quaint bit of pottery and rare piece of silken stuff was exchanged for the Professor's gold and silver. Both consulate and shop were interesting to me, but the people of Tangier claimed much of my attention, and so I paid court to the Arabs.

All these Arabs mind their own business, and are courteous as well as reserved. Later on I went about with my camera, taking photographs in the most crowded streets; but no one noticed me, or paid the slightest attention to my movements. Against the outer walls of the city, near the central gate, an old Arab had spread out a great collection of Moorish knives, swords, long brass-barrelled guns with triangular butts, old clothes, and tarnished ornaments; but all were very dear, and I did not purchase.

The most interesting people here, to me, were the workers in brass. They sat squatted on the mud floors of their shops, stamping out various figures in sheets of brass, making trays and salvers, which were very cheap, ranging from a *peceta* (twenty cents) to a dollar.

Through the market-place we worried our way, pricing various articles and making purchases, — or rather my guide did for me. At every place we stopped, Mahomet made long palaver in Arabic, to which the shopman replied with equal fluency, the result always being that the price was a little more than if I had depended upon my unaided efforts! For Mahomet expected, and he always returned and got, a small fee for every article sold the stranger. This, of course, invariably added to the price, and the stranger had to pay it. As nearly all the shopmen spoke Spanish a little, I really needed no guide, and soon found that I could save money by making my purchases myself.

The second day of my stay in Tangier the great market-place outside the walls was crowded with Arabs from the country, come in to hold a fair, — long trains of camels, troops of horses, and a motley crowd of ragged Bedouins. They pitched their brown tents of goat's-hair in every available spot; they made the filthy place even filthier, and the air was rent with their various cries. All sorts of strolling jugglers and players congregated here, but the chief centre of attraction was the snake-charmer. He was a wild, half-naked Bedouin, with his tangled hair falling over a face in which cunning and ferocity were equally mixed. He had a sack full of snakes, which by a sudden movement he emptied upon the ground. The crowd, that had closely pressed him, quickly scattered, but hemmed him in again when he began to perform. A naked boy sat on the ground, making doleful noises upon a tom-tom, and an old hag sat crouched at his left hand. Taking a large snake in his hand, he bit it in the middle, and then left it free to squirm about his head and shoulders. The reptile darted wildly about, but did not seem to dare to bite, hissing in his face and thrusting out its flaming tongue. Another snake he took and held in front of his face, thrusting out his tongue, at which the snake would dart its own and strive to bite it. Other snakes he coiled about his arms and

SNAKE-CHARMING.

placed in his hair, until he was almost enveloped in writhing reptiles. He did not escape scathless, however, for one of these, a thick-bodied snake with triangular head, bit him on the arm. Instantly ridding himself of the others, he seized this one by the neck and thrust its head into the cavernous jaws of a species of boa, and held it there until the boa had begun to swallow it. Despite the struggles of the victim, it slowly entered the craw of the boa, the distance between the mouth and its tail growing shorter and shorter. A shower of coppers rewarded the charmer for his exhibition, but he gazed at the coin with contempt, and the old hag hobbled about, gathering them in. Another attraction drew the snake-charmer's audience away, and he glared about him until another crowd had collected. All this happened near the *Bab-el-Sok*, or Gate of the Market-place, which is one of the principal gates; the other gate is at the other end of the chief street, and is called *Bab-el-Marsa*, or Gate of the Marine.

The population of Tangier is said to be about fifteen thousand, with about four hundred Europeans. The chief attractions are the market-places, the Kasba, the mosques (which no unbelievers may enter), and the Pasha's palace, where is the harem, which is sometimes shown to ladies, but never to men.

Now and then you may see women in the streets, though rarely, enveloped in white *haiks*. A well-known writer says of Algiers: "Except the changes in artificial landmarks of the country, the greater infusion of the Arabic element into the language of the lowlands, the substitution of the prayers of El Islam for the rites of the Pagan, the adoption of firearms in place of bows and slings, and the use of saddles, the old Numidians and Mauritanians, with Massinissa and Syphax at their head, would now see, could they start from their graves, nothing to excite surprise." All the more is this true of Morocco than of Algiers, where there has been no change in a thousand years.

The kingdom of Morocco is said to contain three hundred

thousand square miles, though it is undefined toward the south, and the least known portion of North Africa. It has mineral deposits of great value, it is thought, but they are unworked. Its backbone is the great Atlas chain of mountains, which rises in peaks as high as ten thousand feet, and in it all the Moroccan rivers take their rise. The aspect of the country varies with the year, from a desert to a garden.

"Drifts of asphodel, white lilies, blue convolvuli, white broom-flowers, thyme and lavender, borage, marigold, purple thistles, colossal daisies and poppies, spread over the hills and plains in the spring in masses acres in extent; but the season of floral splendor is brief." There are opportunities for agriculture, but the people seldom reap "more than will bring the year about."

The population is perhaps six million, of three elements, mainly Berbers, Arabs, Jews. It is probably less populous than it was two thousand years ago. Even to-day some of its cities are *sacred cities*, that no Christian can enter. Its history is here epitomized: Morocco, known to the Romans as Mauritania Tingitana, was conquered by the Vandals, A. D. 429, but recovered to the East by Belisarius. The Arabs penetrated North Africa under Okba, but only conquered and converted the Berbers of Morocco at the time of Musa, in the early part of the eighth century. In the tenth century the Berbers, with the Fatimite caliphs at their head, overthrew and ended forever Arab rule here. Morocco was aggressively active in affairs till the end of the fourteenth century, when Spain and Portugal took its coast cities and subdued its spirit; it again revived, and pursued that career of piracy which has indelibly stamped the nation with opprobrium; but at present it has only the prestige of former greatness, and has no standing in the affairs of nations. In this century the principal events are the abolition of Christian slavery and suppression of piracy, 1822; the defeat of forces sent to aid Abd-el-Kader in Algiers, the bombardment of

JEWS OF TANGIER.

Tangier and Mogador, rout of the Moors at the battle of Isly, and peace of Tangier, 1844; surrender to Spain of the disputed territory of Ceuta, 1845; a Spanish invasion, victory by General O'Donnell, Moors to pay twenty thousand piastres and allow a Spanish mission-house in Fez, 1860; a decree, permitting Europeans to trade in any part of the empire, 1864. The country is under despotic control, the officials in power wringing from the people all the money they can, and justice is only to be obtained in the Turkish way. There are no roads, and travel is unsafe. I found that I could go to Tetuan — an ancient and important city — in a day, if the roads were good; but when I was there the roads were pronounced impassable. To make that short journey I should need — a soldier, as escort, with horse, at one dollar per day; a horse or mule for myself, at the same price; and provender for the journey. There is a hotel in Tetuan, kept by a Hebrew, who is, or was, British vice-consul.

At about nine o'clock one evening Mahomet came for me with a lantern, and we sallied forth. There is not a street-lamp in all Morocco, and every street in Tangier is as dark as Tophet. The sky was clear, and all the stars were sparkling, as I could see by looking up through the rifts in the walls of rock which answered as streets. Everybody carries a lantern when out at night; though Tangier, unlighted as it is, is said to be safer than London or New York. Arabs and donkeys jostled us at every corner, but no one offered an insult. We drifted into an Arab café, where eight Moorish musicians were singing and playing like mad. Their instruments were peculiar, the chiefest being a big-bellied violin, shaped like half a watermelon. They sat cross-legged, on mats, their backs against the wall, and played as fast as they could move their elbows. Two or three of the plaintive songs sung by them were those of the Moors expelled from Andalusia. Coffee and sweetmeats were passed around; then we paid the musicians and departed.

Having signified to Mahomet a desire to gain a peep into a Moorish household, that worthy conducted me to a house in a narrow alley and knocked on the door. An old woman thrust out her face, and seeing Mahomet, opened the door just wide enough for us to enter, then quickly closed it. I found myself in a small apartment with bare walls, at one end a divan covered with silks, upon which reclined a black-eyed maiden *en déshabillé*. A round little youngster rolled on the floor; a dim light flashed over the room from a brass lamp suspended high. It needed but a glance to discover that the damsel was not a Moorish maiden, but an apostate Jewess. She was gracious, though, and did not seem to resent the fact that her unveiled charms could not detain me. *Hasta luego,*— "Until we meet again," she said smilingly; and my adventure was ended. We reached the hotel about midnight.

THE GRAND MOSQUE, TANGIER.

A fine view of the city is had from the Kasba, which caps the apex of the shining hill. The immense walls of this citadel enclose a small town by itself, and there the governor resides, in luxurious quarters. There is a mosque here, and the remains of structures of various epochs. The finest arches and corridors are those of the old Exchange, which is now used as a prison; the miserable beings confined here rarely see light, and are fed by charity.

From the sea we have the best view of Tangier. It covers the slopes of three hills, with a valley between, and the Kasba crowns the southern hill, with its gray walls, white arches, and octagonal minaret. It has crenellated battlements, projecting buttresses, and the remains of towers. The strongest portion is the water battery, below and east of the Kasba, to which strangers are not admitted. A long row of guns *en barbette* surmounts the wall above the mole, and guns peer out at intervals everywhere, but they would be of little service against an armed vessel. The walls are in a very ruinous condition, especially on the landward side, where they are the more picturesque, being in places overgrown with vines and cacti, whose flowers blossom everywhere.

THE MORNING PRAYERS.

Now and then a modern house crops out, but most are peculiar to the country; they are white and creamy-hued. Behind all rises Mount Washington, named in honor of our first President: on either side are green slopes. To the east is a long stretch of sand beach, behind which the pastures and hillside gardens are of a lovely green. The tiles of the mosques and minarets are most of them green, or greenish, with now and then a roof of red.

But the sun has sunk beyond the horizon. From the minaret the muezzin now proclaims the hour of prayer. "Come to prayer! Come to prayer! It is better to pray than to sleep!" As the rosy flush of sunset dies out of the sky, this call to prayer is repeated throughout the city, and rolls over the roof-tops like a great wave, and the day is done.

Gathered together on the roof-top of our hotel, as the muezzin's cry rang over the city, we listened to the Professor as he discoursed upon the early history of Morocco, and the conquest of North Africa by the followers of Mahomet: —

El Hijra — the Flight of Mahomet — occurred A. D. 622, from Mecca to Medina. Mahomet was born about 571, and died 632. Within ninety years, Syria, Persia, and North Africa had been brought under control by his fanatical followers, and an army was gathered at the Pillars of Hercules, ready for the invasion of Spain. Previous to the appearance of Mahomet these Arabians had been idolaters and Nature-worshippers. A holy place, even to the early Arabs, was Zem-zem, the spring in the desert that had miraculously burst forth for the refreshing of Hagar and Ishmael, which finally became their Mek-kah, or place of concourse, where stood the *kaaba*, or temple, within it the black stone said to have fallen from Paradise at the fall of Adam, in a setting of silver, and placed in the northeast corner. Associated with these terms, *Mecca* and *kaaba*, is the *Koran*, the holy book, which Mahomet ingeniously constructed from the Jewish history and the Jewish prophets, drawing distinctions without differences. The prophets (according to Mahomet) are Adam, Seth, Noah, Abraham, Moses, Jesus — and Mahomet. Islamism insists, first, upon belief in God, in angels, in the Koran, in the prophets, in predestination. At Mahomet's death there were two rivals, Ali, his cousin and son-in-law, husband of Fatima, and Abu Bekr, father of his favorite wife, Ayesha, and who was elected caliph. The various sects and schisms date from this division. An army of conquest was sent into Syria, and Damascus was taken A. D. 634. Cairo (*El Kahira*, City of Victory) also fell before the fanatics, then Alexandria, in 640, and six million Copts are said to have submitted voluntarily and adopted the religion of their conquerors. Then (as we know) was burned the famous Library of Alexandria, according to the decree of Omar: "If these writings of the Greeks agree with the Koran, they are useless, and need not be preserved; if they disagree, they are pernicious, and ought to be destroyed." In this connection, let me note that the blood-stained copy of the Koran held by Othman (who was beheaded 650) is said to have been later found in the mosque of Cordova, in Spain.

The Caliphate was removed to Damascus, 673, and thence the Moslem armies were sent out east and west under Sezid to Constantinople, and Obah was made governor of Africa. North Africa at that time went by its Roman names, such as Numidia, Mauritania, Tingitania, Morocco. A trusted general named Musa (Moses) was appointed to command in Eastern Africa, and his armies quickly conquered the Berbers, who flocked by thousands to his banner and his religion. Mosques were built, with their *kibbah*, or holy niche, toward the east, toward Mecca, and the minaret at the other end, whence the muezzin shouted the call to prayer: "Great God! Great God! There is no God except God!"

In the early years of the eighth century, under Al Walid, caliph of Damascus, Islamism "was established from the banks of the Ganges to the surges of the Atlantic." Musa was made Emir of Africa and supreme commander of the Moslems in the west. He had under him six noble sons, one of whom finally took Tangier, — the *Tingis* of the Romans, called by the Arabs *Tanjah*, — command over which was given to Tarik Ibu Zeyad Ibu Abdillah, the Tarik who invaded Spain, and whose name is preserved in the rock of Gibraltar, — *Gib-el-Tarik*. But at Tangier the Arab armies gathered, and this key to the strait was made the *point d'appui* for the invasion of Andalus. The Arab armies gathered restlessly at Tangier. "For more than three quarters of a century conquerors, they were burning for greater conquests; they were soldiers, and the sons of soldiers."

The Arabians, then, were the people who in the early years of the eighth century brought all Spain under Moslem rule, and they were aided by such others of the African tribes as had been converted to their faith. Their mainspring of action may be found in their religion, the faith of Islam, or resignation to the will of God. This, as they interpreted it, made it incumbent upon them to bring everybody outside their fold to their way of thinking, — whether dead or alive it mattered little to the Mahometans. As this religion, Islamism, wrought such changes in the north of Africa as well as throughout the Orient, let us glance at its articles of faith.

"*Monotheism* was its keystone, and *predestination* its supporting columns." *La I'laka illa Allah, Muhammed resoul Allah,* — "There is no God but Allah, and Muhammed is the prophet of Allah." Upon the walls of the Alhambra to-day we find inscriptions conveying similar meanings. These Moslems were Unitarians, with a reservation in favor of Mahomet as the prophet of their God. They early cast aside the images of their ancestors, and were less given to their worship than the Jews, or even the Romanists.

All good Mahometans are strictly enjoined to prayer, almsgiving, fasting, and the pilgrimage to Mecca. Although in Algiers the Moslems do not seem to live strictly up to their faith, yet they are supposed to pray at least four times in twenty-four hours, — at *Azohbi*, before sunrise; *Adokar*, just after meridian; *Almagreb*, before sunset; *Alaksa*, in the evening. You may yet hear the muezzin admonishing the people from the minaret: "Come to prayers! Come to prayers! It is better to pray than to sleep!"

The angels were believed to be creatures of light, and there were four archangels, — Gabriel (*Jebriel*), Michael (*Mechal*), Azrael (the messenger of death), and Israfael (sounder of the resurrection trump). In addition to these there was *Eblis*, or the devil.

A stranger who had preceded us describes perhaps better than we can the Arab cities of Tangier and Morocco: —

"Coming out upon the only square that Tangier can boast, which is cut by one long street that begins at the shore and crosses the whole town, you see a rectangular place surrounded by shops that would be mean in the poorest of our villages. On one side there is a fountain constantly surrounded by blacks and Arabs drawing water in jars and gourds; on the other side sit all day long on the ground eight or ten muffled women selling bread. Around this square are the very modest houses of the different Legations, which rise like palaces from the midst of the confused multitude of Moorish huts. Here is concentrated all the life of Tangier, — the life of a large village. The one tobacconist is here, the one apothecary, the one café, — a dirty room with a billiard-table, — and the one solitary corner where a printed notice may sometimes be seen. Here gather the half-naked street-boys, the rich and idle Moorish gentlemen, Jews talking about their business, Arab porters awaiting the arrival of the steamer, attachés of the Legations expecting the dinner-hour, travellers just arrived, interpreters, and impostors of various kinds. The courier arriving from Fez or Morocco with orders from the Sultan is to be met

ARAB WOMAN OF TANGIER.

here, and the servant coming from the post with his hands full of journals from London and Paris; the beauty of the harem and the wife of the minister; the Bedouin's camel and the lady's lapdog; the turban and the chimney-pot hat ; and the sound of a piano from the windows of a consulate mingles with the lamentable chant from the door of a mosque.

This country, shut in by the Mediterranean, Algeria, the Desert of Sahara, and the ocean, crossed by the great chain of the Atlas, bathed by wide rivers, opening into immense plains, with every variety of climate, endowed with inestimable riches in all the three kingdoms of Nature, destined by its position to be the great commercial high-road between Europe and Central Africa, is now occupied by about eight million of inhabitants, — Berbers, Moors, Arabs, Jews, Negroes, and Europeans, sprinkled over a vaster extent of country than that of France. The Berbers, who form the basis of the indigenous population, — a savage, turbulent, and indomitable race, — live on the inaccessible mountains of the Atlas, in almost complete independence of the Imperial authority. The Arabs, the conquering race, occupy the plains, — a nomadic and pastoral people, not entirely degenerated from their ancient haughty character. The Moors, corrupted and crossed by Arab blood, are in great part descended from the Moors of Spain, and inhabiting the cities, hold in their hands the wealth, trade, and commerce of the country. The blacks, about five hundred thousand, originally from the Soudan, are generally servants, laborers, and soldiers. The Jews, almost equal in number to the blacks, are descended for the most part from those who were exiled from Europe in the Middle Ages, and are more oppressed, hated, degraded, and persecuted here than in any other country in the world. They exercise various arts and trades, and in a thousand ways display the ingenuity, pliability, and tenacity of their race, finding in the possessions torn from their oppressors a recompense for all their woes. The Europeans, whom Mussulman intolerance has little by little driven from the interior of the empire toward the coast, number less than two thousand in all Morocco, the greater part inhabiting Tangier, and living under the protection of the consular flags.

This heterogeneous, dispersed, and irreconcilable population is oppressed rather than protected by military government that, like a monstrous leech, sucks out all the vital juice from the State. The tribes and boroughs, or suburbs, obey their sheiks, the cities and provinces the cadi, the greater province the pasha, and the pasha obeys the Sultan, — grand scherif, high-priest, and supreme judge, executor of the laws emanating from himself, free to change at his caprice money, taxes, weights, and measures, master of the possessions and the lives of his subjects. Under the weight of this government, and within the inflexible circle of the Mussulman religion, unmoved by European influence, and full of a savage fanaticism, everything that in other countries moves and progresses, here remains motionless or falls into ruin. Commerce is choked by monopolies, by prohibitions upon exports and imports, and by the capricious mutability of the laws. Manufactures, restricted by the bonds laid upon commerce, have remained as they were at the time of the expulsion of the Moors from Spain, with the same primitive tools and methods. Agriculture, loaded heavily with taxes, hampered in exportation of produce, and only exercised from sheer necessity, has fallen so low as no longer to merit the name. Science, suffocated by the Koran, and contaminated by superstition, is reduced to a few elements in the higher schools, such as were taught in the Middle Ages. There are no printing-presses, no books, no journals, no geographical maps; the language itself, a corruption of the Arabic, and represented only by an imperfect and variable written character, is becoming yearly more debased; in the general decadence the national character is corrupted; all the ancient Mussulman civilization is disappearing. Morocco, the last western bulwark of Islamism, once the seat of a monarchy that ruled from the Ebro to the Soudan, and from the Niger to the Balearic Isles, glorious with flourishing university, with immense libraries, with men famous for their learning, with formidable fleets and armies, is now nothing but a small and almost unknown State, full of wretchedness and ruin, resisting with its last remaining strength the advance of European civilization, seated upon its foundation still, but confronted by the reciprocal jealousies of civilized States. As for Tangier, the ancient Tingis, which gave its name to Tingitania Mauritania, it passed successively from the hands of the Romans into those of the Vandals, Greeks, Visigoths, Arabs, Portuguese, and English, and is now a city of about fifteen thousand inhabitants, considered by its sister cities as having been "prostituted to the Christian," although there are no Christian churches in it.

PRINCIPAL STREET OF TANGIER.

CHAPTER III.

A CARAVAN JOURNEY TO FEZ.—THE POWDER-PLAY, AND THE SULTAN.

JOURNEYING through Morocco is not considered safe, for Christians have ever in mind that it is inculcated in the Koran that "to kill a Christian will entitle a Mahometan to free transportation to heaven, in company with ten houris as attendants;" and there are a great many Arabs desirous of taking the trip in just such company.

To reach the great city of Fez, it would be necessary to take a week, and would cost about one hundred and fifty dollars, as a large escort is considered necessary. We were determined to make the journey, notwithstanding the fatigue and expense; and finding a party of French and Italian travellers about to set out, we obtained permission to join them.

One lovely day, when all the fields about Tangier were bright and blooming, we filed out of the Market Gate, the *Bab-el-Sok*, and took our way over the plains. As we did not pass through many towns on the route, I shall confine myself to narrating some of the interesting incidents by the way. We had a large escort, for our mission was a semi-official one, and soldiers are cheap in Morocco. The Doctor and I had each a splendid stallion of Arab blood; but the Professor preferred a donkey, because he could be nearer the ground and could see the plants, minerals, and land-shells all the better as he went along. The Arab officers laughed at him as

they pranced past on their magnificent horses, but the Professor
didn't mind; and as for the rest of us, we had all we could do
to manage our own spirited steeds. One of the finest exhibitions of
the journey was the celebrated Powder-Play, and as it is described
by the Italian, I give it in his words: —

"Then began one of the most splendid *lab-el-barada* (or powder-plays)
that could be desired. They charged in couples, by tens, one by one, in the

AMUSEMENTS ON THE JOURNEY.

bottom of the valley, on the hills, in front and at the sides of the caravan,
forward and backward, firing and yelling without cessation. In a few minutes the valley was as full of the smoke and smell of powder as a battle-
field. On every side horses pranced and glittered, mantles floated, and red,
yellow, green, blue, and orange caftans mingled with the shine of sabres and
poniards. One by one they darted by like winged phantoms, old and young,

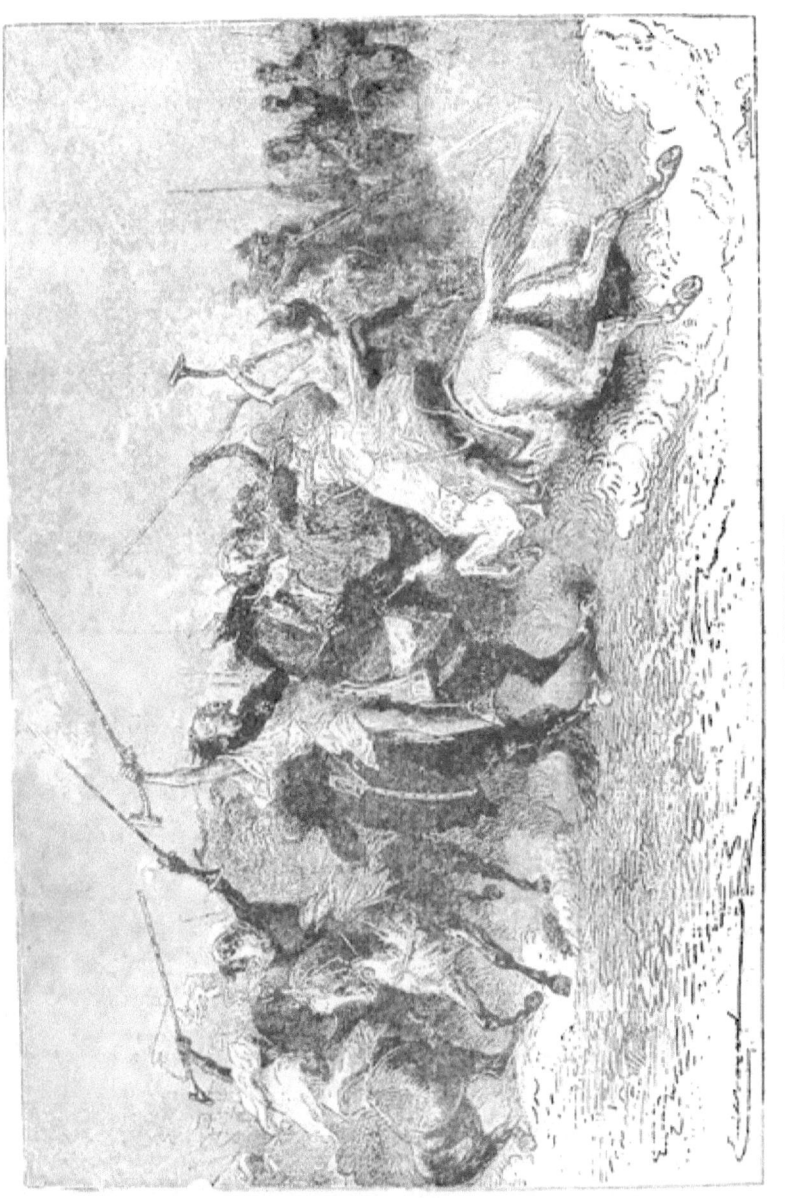

THE POWDER-PLAY.

men of colossal proportion, strange and terrible figures, erect in their stirrups, with heads thrown back, hair streaming in the wind, and muskets held aloft; and each as he discharged his piece gave a savage cry, which the interpreter translated for us: 'Have a care!' 'Oh, my mother!' 'In the name of God!' 'I kill thee!' 'Thou art dead!' 'I am avenged!' Some dedicated the shot to a special purpose or person: 'To my master.' 'To my horse.' 'To my dead.' 'To my sweetheart.' They fired up and down and behind, bending and twisting as though they had been tied to the saddle. Here and there one would lose his mantle or his turban, and he would turn in full career and pick it up with the point of his musket. Some threw their guns up in the air and caught them as they fell. Their looks and gestures were like those of men mad with drink, and risking their lives in a sort of joyful fury. Most of the horses dripped blood from their bellies, and the feet and stirrups and extremities of the mantles of the riders were all bloody. Some faces in the multitude impressed themselves upon my memory from the first, — among others, a young man with a cyclopean head and an immense pair of shoulders, dressed in a rose-colored caftan, and who emitted a succession of roars like those of a wounded lion; a lad of fifteen, handsome, bareheaded, and all in white, who passed three times, crying, 'My God! my God!' a long, bony old man, with a most ill-omened visage, who flew by with half-shut eyes and a satanic grin upon his face, as if he carried the plague behind him; a black, all eyes and teeth, with a monstrous scar across his forehead, who writhed furiously about in his saddle, as if to free himself from the clutch of some invisible hand.

"In this fashion they accompanied the march of the caravan, ascending and descending the heights, forming groups, dissolving and reforming, with every combination of color, till they seemed like the fluttering of a myriad of banners."

With such scenes as this our time passed merrily. Everything was strange and new to us. At night tents were pitched and we slept on the ground, our heads pillowed on our saddles; by day, we travelled on. The air was pure, the sun bright, and altogether it was a joyous journey. At the end of the sixth day, as it was time to pitch our camps, we caught sight of the minarets of Fez, the capital of Morocco. Next morning, with banners flying and wild riding Arabs discharging their muskets, we entered the sacred city.

"The city extends in the form of a monstrous figure eight, between two hills, upon which still tower the ruins of two ancient fortifications. Beyond the hills there is a chain of mountains. The Pearl River divides the town in two, — modern Fez on the left bank, ancient Fez on the right; and a girdle of old castellated walls and towers, dark and falling into ruin, binds the whole together. From the heights the eye takes in the whole city, — a myriad of white, flat-roofed houses, among which rise tall minarets ornamented with mosaics, gigantic palm-trees, tufts of verdure, green domes, and castellated towers. The grandeur of the ancient city can be divined from what is left, though it is but a skeleton. Near the gates, and upon the hills, for a long distance the country is covered with monuments and ruins, tombs and houses of the saints, arches of aqueducts, sepulchres, *zanie*, and foundations that seem like the remains of a city destroyed by cannon and devoured by flames. Between the wall and the highest of the two hills that flank the city it is all one garden; a thick and intricate grove of mulberry-trees, olives, palms, fruit-trees, and tall poplars, clothed with ivy and grape-vines, intersect it between high green banks. The opposite bank is crowned with aloes twice the height of a man. Along the walls are great fissures and deep ditches filled with vegetation, rude remains of bastions and broken towers, — a grand and severe disorder of ruin and greenery, recalling the picturesque parts of the walls of Constantinople. We passed by the Gate of Ghisa, the Iron Gate, the New Gate, the Burned Gate, the Gate that Opens, the Gate of the Lions, the Gate of Sidi Busida, the Gate of the Father of Utility, and re-entered New Fez by the Gate of the Niche of Butter. Here are large gardens, vast open spaces, large squares surrounded by battlemented walls beyond which can be seen other squares and other walls, arched gateways and towers, and beautiful prospects of hills and mountains. Some of the doors are very lofty, and are covered with iron plates studded with large nails. Our greatest desire, after our first walk about Fez, was to visit the two famous mosques of El-Carnin and Muley-Ednis; but as Christians are not permitted to put a foot in them, we were obliged to content ourselves with what we could see from the street, — the Mosaic doors, the arched courts, the long low aisles divided by a forest of columns and lighted by a dim mysterious light. It must not be imagined, however, that these mosques are now what they were in the time of their fame, since in the fifteenth century the celebrated historian Abd-er-Rhaman-ebu-Kaldun, describing that of El-Carnin (may God exalt it more and more, as he says), speaks of various ornaments that were no longer in existence in his time. The foundation of this enormous mosque was laid on the first Saturday of Ramadan, in the year 859 of Jesus Christ, at the expense of a

INTERIOR OF A MOORISH MOSQUE.

pious woman of Kairwan. It was at the beginning a small mosque of four naves; but, little by little, governors, emirs, and sultans embellished and enlarged it. Upon the point of the minaret built by the Imaun-Ahmed-ben Aby-Beker glittered a golden ball studded with pearls and precious stones, on which was represented the sword of Ednis-ebu-Ednis, the founder of Fez. On the interior walls were suspended talismans, which protected the mosque against rats, scorpions, and serpents. The *Mirab*, or niche, turned toward Mecca was so splendid that the Imaun had it painted white, that it might no longer distract the faithful from their prayers. There was a pulpit of ebony, inlaid with ivory and gems. There were two hundred and seventy columns, forming sixteen naves of twenty-one arches, in each; fifteen great doors of entrance for the men, and two small ones for the women; and seventeen hundred hanging lamps, which in the season of Ramadan consumed three quintals and a half of oil, — all which particulars the historian Kaldun relates with exclamations of wonder and delight, adding that the mosque could contain twenty-two thousand and seven hundred, and that the court alone had in its pavement fifty-two thousand bricks. 'Glory to Allah, Lord of the world, immensely merciful, and king of the day of the last judgment!'"

Quarters were assigned us at a caravansary; but we were everywhere looked upon with suspicion, and required an escort of soldiers whenever we moved abroad. An eventful day was that in which we saw the Sultan when he received the Italian ambassador.

"He was on horseback, followed by a throng of courtiers on foot, one of whom held over his head an immense parasol. At a few paces from the ambassador he stopped his horse; a portion of his suite closed the square, the rest grouped themselves about him. The master of ceremonies with knotty stick shouted in a loud voice, 'The ambassador from Italy!' The ambassador, accompanied by his interpreter, advanced with uncovered head. The Sultan said in Arabic, 'Welcome! Welcome! Welcome!' Then he asked if he had had a good journey, and if he were content with the service of the escort, and with the reception of the governors. But of all this we heard nothing; we were fascinated. The Sultan, whom our imagination had represented to us under the aspect of a cruel and savage despot, was the handsomest and most charming young fellow that had ever excited the fancy of an *odalisque*. He is tall and slender, with large soft eyes, a fine aquiline nose, and his dark visage is of a perfect oval, encircled by a short black beard, — a noble face, full of sadness and gentleness. A mantle of snowy whiteness fell from his head to his feet; his turban was covered by a tall hood; his feet were bare, except for yellow slippers and golden stirrups. All this whiteness and amplitude of grace and affability corresponded admirably with the expression of his face. The parasol, sign of command, which a courtier held a little inclined behind him, — a great, round parasol, three meters in height, lined with blue silk embroidered with gold, and covered on the outside with amaranth, topped by a great golden ball, — added to the dignity of his appearance. His graceful action, his smiling and pensive expression, his low voice, sweet and monotonous as the murmur of a stream, his whole person and manners, had something of ingenuous and feminine, and at the same time solemn, that inspired irresistible sympathy and profound respect.

"This great curiosity was produced in part by the history of his dynasty. There was the wish to look in the face of one of that terrible family of the Scherifs Fileli, to whom history assigns pre-eminence in fanaticism, ferocity, and crime, over all the dynasties than have ever reigned in Morocco. At the beginning of the seventeenth century some inhabitants of Tafilet, a province of the empire on the confines of the desert, the Scherifs of which take the name of Fileli, brought from Morocco into their country a Scherif named Ali, a native of Jambo, and a descendant of Mahomet by Hassen, the second son of Ali and Fatima. The climate of the province of Tafilet, a little after his arrival, resumed a mildness that it had for some time lost; dates grew in great abundance. The merit was attributed to Ali; Ali was elected king under the name of Muley-Scherif; his descendants gradually, by aid of their arms, extended the kingdom of their ancestor; they took possession of Morocco and Fez, drove out the dynasty of the Saadini-Scherifs, and have reigned up to our day over the whole country comprised between the Muluia, the desert, and the sea.

"Sidi-Mohammed, son of Muley-Scherif, reigned with wise clemency, but after him the throne was steeped in blood. El Reschid governed by terror, usurped the office of executioner, and lacerated with his own hands the breasts of women in order to force them to reveal the hiding-places of their husbands' treasure. Muley-Ismial, the luxurious prince, the lover of eight thousand women, father of twelve hundred sons, and founder of the famous corps of black guards, was the gallant Sultan who asked in marriage of Louis XIV. the daughter of the Duchesse de la Vallière, and stuck ten thousand heads over the battlements of Morocco and Fez. Muley-Ahmed-el-Dehedi, avaricious and a debauchee, stole the jewels of his father's women, stupefied himself with wine, pulled out the teeth of his own wives, and cut off the head

AN OFFICER OF THE MOORISH LEGATION.

of a slave who had pressed the tobacco too much down into his pipe. Muley-Abdallah, vanquished by the Berbers, cut the throats of the inhabitants of Mechinez to satisfy his rage, aided the executioner in decapitating the officers of his brave but vanquished army, and invented the horrible torture of cooking a man alive inside a disembowelled bull, that the two might purify together.

"The best of the race appears to have been Sidi-Mohammed, his son, who surrounded himself with renegade Christians, tried to live at peace, and brought Morocco nearer to Europe. Then came Muley-Yezid, a cruel and violent fanatic, who in order to pay his soldiers gave them leave to sack and pillage the Hebrew quarters in all the cities of the empire; Muley-Hescham, who after a reign of a few days went into sanctuary to die; Muley-Soliman, who destroyed piracy, and made a show of friendship to Europe, but with artful

FEATS OF HORSEMANSHIP.

cunning separated Morocco from all civilized States, and caused to be brought to the foot of his throne the heads of all renegade Jews from whom had escaped a word of regret for their forced abjuration; Abd-er-Raman, the conqueror of Isly, who built up conspirators alive into the walls of Fez; and finally, Sidi-Mohammed, the victor of Tetuan, who in order to inculcate respect and devotion in his people sent the heads of his enemies to the *duars* and cities, stuck upon his soldiers' muskets.

"Nor are these the worst calamities that afflicted the empire under the fatal dynasty of the Fileli. There are wars with Spain, Holland, Portugal, England, France, and the Turks of Algiers; ferocious insurrections of Berbers, disastrous expeditions into the Soudan; revolts of fanatical tribes; mutinies of the black guard; persecutions of the Christians; furious wars of succession between father and son, uncle and nephew, brother and brother; the empire by turns dismembered and rejoined; Sultans five times discrowned and five times reinstated; unnatural vengeance of princes of the same blood, jealousies and horrid crimes, and monstrous suffering, and precipitate decline into antique barbarism; and at all times one principle is triumphant, — that not being able to admit European civilization unless upon the ruins of the entire political and religious edifice of the Prophet, ignorance is the best bulwark of the empire, and barbarism an element necessary to its life."

TRAVELLING IN MOROCCO.

CHAPTER IV.

MOROCCO AND THE MOORS.

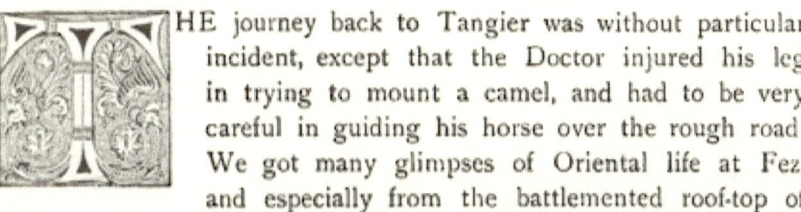HE journey back to Tangier was without particular incident, except that the Doctor injured his leg in trying to mount a camel, and had to be very careful in guiding his horse over the rough road. We got many glimpses of Oriental life at Fez, and especially from the battlemented roof-top of the house in which we were domiciled. It is forbidden to strangers to behold the Moorish women except they are closely veiled; but now and then we had the privilege without the fair sex being aware of it.

"Looking through those loop-holed windows, we seemed to see into another world. Upon the terraces far and near were many women, the greater part of them, judging by their dress, in easy circumstances, — ladies, if that title can be given to Moorish women. A few were seated upon the parapets, — some walking about, some jumping with the agility of squirrels from one terrace to the other, hiding, reappearing, and throwing water in one another's faces, laughing merrily. There were old women and young, and little girls of eight or ten, all dressed in the strangest garments, and of the most brilliant colors. Most of them had their hair falling over their shoulders, a red or green silk handkerchief tied round the head in a band, a sort of caftan of different colors, with wide sleeves, bound round the waist with blue or crimson sash; a velvet jacket open at the breast; wide trousers, yellow slippers, and large silver rings above the ankle. The slaves and children had nothing on but a chemise. One only of these ladies was near enough for us to see her features. She was a woman of about thirty, dressed in gala dress, and standing on a terrace a cat's jump below our own. She was looking down into a garden, leaning her head upon her hand. We looked at her with a glass. Heavens! what a picture! Eyes dark with antimony, cheeks painted red, throat painted white, nails stained with henna, she was a perfect painter's palette, but handsome, despite her thirty years, with a full face, almond-shaped eyes, languid, and veiled by long

A SOLITARY TREE ON THE PLAIN.

black lashes, the nose a little turned up, a small round mouth, as the Moorish poet says, like a ring, and a sylph-like figure whose soft and curving lines were shown by the thin texture of her dress. She seemed sad. Perhaps some fourth bride of fourteen had lately entered the harem and stolen her husband's

A SCENE IN MOROCCO

caresses. From time to time she glanced at her hand, her arm, a tress of hair that fell over her bosom, and sighed. The sound of our voices suddenly roused her. She looked up, saw that we were observing her, jumped over the parapet of the terrace with the dexterity of an acrobat, and vanished."

ON THE COAST OF MOROCCO.

The early age at which the Moorish children (for they are little more than children) marry surprised us. A Moorish mother and her daughter came into the court one day, and we greatly admired the childlike face and pretty manners of the little lady. We asked how old she was. "Twelve years old," the mother said. "She will soon be married," we remarked. "*Che!*" exclaimed the mother, "she is *too old* to marry." We all thought she was joking. But she repeated, almost astonished at our incredulity, "I speak the truth; look here at this one," and she pointed to a smaller child. "She will be ten in six months, and she has already been married one year." The child held down her head. We were still incredulous. "What can I say?" continued the woman. "If you will not believe my word, do me the honor to come to my house on

Saturday, so that we may receive you worthily, and you will see the husband and the witnesses of the marriage." "And how old is the husband?" I asked. "Ten years old, Signore." Seeing that we still doubted, the other women all asserted the same, adding that it is quite rare for a girl to marry after twelve years of age; that the greater part of them are married at ten, many at eight, and some even at seven, to boys of about their own age; and that, naturally, while they are so young, they live with their parents, who continue to treat them like children, feed, clothe, and correct them, without the least regard to their marital dignity; but they are always together, and the wife is submissive to the husband.

The absolute power of the Sultan over his subjects was well illustrated by a scene an Englishman witnessed one day in the great market-place. It seems that two men had committed some political offence, and were sentenced to have their heads cut off. They were taken to the market-place, and a miserable wretch was hired to do the business. Just as he was about to begin (to quote from the Englishman)

"An altercation broke out between the soldiers and the executioner about the reward promised for decapitation of the two poor creatures, who stood by and listened to the dispute over the blood-money. The executioner insisted, declaring that he had been promised twenty francs a head, and must have forty for the two. The officer at last agreed, but with a very ill grace. Then the butcher seized one of the condemned men, already half dead with terror, threw him on the ground, kneeling on his chest, and put the knife to his throat. The Englishman turned away his face. He heard the sounds of a violent struggle. The executioner cried out, 'Give me another knife; mine does not cut!' Another knife was brought, and the head separated from the body. The soldiers cried in a faint voice, 'God prolong the life of our lord and master!' But many of them were stupefied with terror.

"Then came another victim, a handsome and amiable-looking young man. Again they wrangled over his blood. The officer, denying his promise, declaring he would give but twenty francs for both heads, the butcher was forced to yield. The condemned asked that his hands might be unbound. Being loosed, he took his cloak and gave it to the soldier who had unbound him, saying, 'Accept this; we shall meet in a better world.' He threw his turban to another, who had been looking at him with compassion, and stepping to the place where lay the bloody corpse of his companion, he said in a clear, firm voice, 'There is no God but God, and Mahomet is His prophet!' Then taking off his belt he gave it to the executioner, saying, 'Take it; but for the love of God cut my head off more quickly than you did my brother's.' He stretched himself on the earth in the blood, and the executioner kneeled upon his breast. 'A reprieve, stop!' cried the Englishman. A horseman came galloping toward them. The executioner held his knife suspended. 'It is only the governor's son,' said a soldier. 'He is coming to see the execution. Wait for him.' So it was indeed. A few minutes after, two bleeding heads were held up by the soldiers.

A RAPID GAIT.

Then the gates of the city were opened, and there came forth a crowd of boys, who pursued the executioner for three miles, when he fell fainting to the ground, covered with wounds. The next day it was known that he had been shot by a relative of one of the victims, and buried where he fell. The authorities of Tangier apparently did not trouble themselves about the matter, since the assassin came back into the city and remained unmolested. After having been exposed three days, the heads were sent to the Sultan, in order that his Imperial Majesty might recognize the promptitude with which his orders had been fulfilled. The soldiers who were carrying

A MOORISH FESTIVAL.

them met on their way a courier bearing a pardon, who had been detained by the sudden flooding of a river!"

It was in Morocco that we caught glimpses of the Bedouin Arab on his native plains. Like the Arab of Algiers, he has never changed his habits or his costume, presenting the same savage aspect and leading the same wild and roving life that his ancestors did. As in olden time, his hand is against every one, and everybody's hand is now and then turned against him. The Professor made a special study of the Arab as we went along, and the following is the result of his observations:—

"Each hut or tent shelters an entire family. A group of huts is called a *dechera*, or hamlet; if composed of tents, it takes the name of *douar*. They wear the costume of the Berbers, and in addition, sometimes the *haik*, a long piece of very light cloth, first wrapped around the body, then brought around the head, where it is kept in place by a camel's-hair cord. On great occasions the horsemen wear horse-boots of red leather.

"All the Arabs live in tents, and are nomads. Their food consists of *cous-cous*, of wheat or barley, the various fruits, especially dates of the desert, of which they are extremely fond, mutton when they can get it, and milk. They are very frugal, and more temperate than other natives. The city dwellers have adopted a more complicated costume, consisting of *bouffard* trousers, a broad red belt of wool or silk, a closed waistcoat, and a jacket of cloth or silk; on the feet, shoes without heels, or with the quarters turned in; on the head, two caps, one of cotton, the other of red wool, placed over the first; over the shoulders a light *burnous*. The native women of the towns are often as light as European brunettes, losing the dark color they had in the country; and this change is so marked that one would be likely to consider them a separate race. They lead a more comfortable life than the country-women, and even if they are deprived of the privilege of going out with uncovered faces, they find some compensation for this in dressing the more coquettishly. Their costume differs from that of the men only by its elegance; the belt is more graceful, the jacket of richer material, the coarse shirt of the men replaced by a garment of gauze, and the scanty waistcoat forms a bodice open at the throat. The coiffure alone is entirely different; the hair is brought to the top of the head, and around it is twisted a fringed silk handkerchief. The young girls braid their hair into one long plait, and wear a sort of velvet cap adorned with sequins. Out of doors

THE CITY OF MOROCCO.

the women wear a little veil which hides all the face below the eyes, while a large piece of cloth falls around the body, hiding its general shape.

"The most elegant houses differ little in furnishing from the tent; carpets, mats, and small mattresses serve as seats during the day and as beds at night. The jewels and gala dresses are piled up in trunks of native wood. Among the poor the meals are served on the ground; among the rich on a copper tray, placed on a very low and small table. Everybody eats from the same dish, — the solid food with the fingers, the liquid with wooden spoons. The men are served first, while the women eat by themselves what is left. Politeness demands that the host, no matter what his rank may be, should himself serve the guest; he first tastes the dishes before presenting them to him; he points out the best morsels to his guest, and if he hesitates to take them he puts them into his mouth.

ARABIAN TRAVELLERS.

"When the *douar* receives a distinguished guest, the repast is furnished by the whole community. The inhabitants of the *douar* then arrange themselves around the guest in a series of concentric circles, graduated by rank. Each dish, after having been tasted by the guest, is served successively to the different circles, and the bones, carefully gnawed, are finally given to the dogs, who are silently though expectantly watching proceedings, and form the outermost circle. All natives have an abiding faith in amulets as a means of preserving health. They are composed of small scraps of paper, on which are traced a few cabalistic signs and words from the Koran. The natives of the town are more given to ablution than the Arabs, the latter being extremely filthy.

"The children of all the Algerian races are extremely precocious, and very intelligent, but their development is early arrested, and the intellectual faculties weaken rapidly. The inferior condition of the native women, which aids in the transmission by heredity of many faults, plays an important part in the tendency to degeneration. They never receive any intellectual culture. They rarely are acquainted with anything beyond their own *douar*, and their intelligence is rapidly consumed, from having to concentrate itself on a restricted circle of vulgar ideas. The men never condescend to converse with the women, and no woman is allowed conversation with strangers.

A SOLDIER OF MOROCCO.

"For these aborigines human society reaches no farther than their own *douar*. They concentrate all their attention on their little world, which is well calculated to inspire in them a brutal egotism, and to give them a mean conception of humanity. Universal ignorance prevails, except that every little community is likely to have its *thaleb*, or scholar, learned enough to read a little of the Koran. The Moslem religion is far from being in a pure state in Algeria. There is no tribe but has its favorite saint, to the tomb of which the people repair constantly to pray. The body of the saint is sheltered by a domed chapel, called *koubba*, in the middle a catafalque covered with silk and brocaded stuffs, the walls hung with banners of silk and native offerings. Sometimes these *koubbas* merely cover the spot where a saint has passed the night. The natives are very superstitious, and fear the evil eye, not only for themselves, but their cattle. The numerous idiots met with there are objects of great attention because they are supposed to be possessed of a devil whom it is prudent to propitiate."

Says another observer: —

"Seeing them eat, I understood how it was that the Moors could do without knives and forks. The neatness and dexterity, the precision with which they pulled chickens, mutton, game, and fish to pieces cannot be described. With a few rapid movements of the hands, without the least discomposure, each one took his exact portion. They seemed to have nails as sharp as razors. They dipped their fingers in the sauces, made balls of the *cuscussu*, ate salad by the handful, and not a morsel or crumb fell from the dish; and when they rose, we saw that their caftans were immaculate. Every now and then a servant carried round a basin and a towel; they gave themselves a wash, and then all together plunged their paws into the next dish. No one spoke, no one raised his eyes, no one seemed to notice that any one was looking on."

A MOORISH BAND OF MUSIC.

The general costume of the Arabs is, first, a long shirt without a collar, descending to the middle of the leg, and with sleeves large as those on a surplice; above this a *haik*, made of silk or linen, which envelops body and breast, and winds the head in five or six folds, where it is retained in place by a white or brown cord of camel's-hair. Outside of all this, sometimes, the Arabs and Moors of quality wear two or three burnouses. When an Arab is mourning the loss of a near relative, he never washes body or clothes for a long period. The nearer the relative deceased, the dirtier the Arab becomes. Our soldiers guarding the caravan were a trifle more cleanly than the wild Arabs, but by no means inviting; so that we welcomed with joy, one afternoon, the announcement that in the distance rose the minarets of Tangier.

CHAPTER V.

SOME TIME IN A PIRATE CITY.

TANGIER again, at last. There we rested several days, and there we gathered up the fragmentary bits of information that we now weave into this story of our journeyings. The American consul was very friendly to us, and showed us a large collection of ancient arms and armor. At that time he was engaged in effecting the release of a lot of Jewish prisoners who had languished for many years in the common prison on charge of debt. We photographed the group, just as they were released, and a most miserable and emaciated crowd they were. One day, as we were passing the open door of a low but massive-walled building, — for doors are always open there, in that favored land where there is no winter, — we heard voices, loud and excited and angry. One voice, we were sure, was that of a countryman of ours, — an American, — and we instinctively halted.

"You're a confounded old blockhead!" it said. "Haven't I been reasoning with you now these three hours, and haven't I been speaking so loud that my lungs are sore, and *yet* you won't understand? I'd give a hundred dollars, this instant, if I could find somebody speaking your outlandish lingo."

It was enough to us that a human being stood in need of assistance, and we made bold to enter the doorway.

"I am at your service, sir," I said. "Do you need an interpreter?"

The speaker we had interrupted was a large, burly, whiskered mariner, clad in an irreproachable suit of linen duck, and excitedly waving a veritable Panama in one hand, in front of a very red and heated face. In front of him stood the man at whom he had launched his heavy thunderbolts, — a slender, dark-featured Spaniard, with coal-black eyes and mustache, and with his shoulders elevated and hands spread in deprecatory protest at the captain's actions. There was an instant change in their respective positions as I entered; the Spaniard ran up to me and embraced me, telling me how much he would be obliged if I would explain things to this masterful *marinaro;* while the large man ceased fanning himself with his hat, and looked at me in open-mouthed astonishment. Recovering himself, he looked as though he would like to follow the impulsive Spaniard's example, and hug us all on the spot. But he compromised by seizing my hand and pressing it between his two brawny fists. It will not be reported what he began his greeting with, but it was sufficiently condemnatory of himself, by himself, to satisfy the most exacting martinet in marine etiquette.

NATIVES OF MOROCCO.

"Bless my heart, young man!" he broke forth explosively; "where in the name of Uncle Sam did you rain down from? I did n't believe there was a man speaking my own tongue in this miserable city. If I had, perhaps I would n't have been so ha'sh about offering a hundred for an interpreter; but I 'll give it to you, just the same. It 'll be worth that to the owners of my vessel."

"Oh, I don't want the money, and I shall feel very glad if I can help you in any trouble."

"You can just do that, my young friend, right here. Don Mariano and I can't understand anything about the manifest; it might make a thousand dollars difference to me, — or to my owners, and that 's the same thing, — and you 've come just in the nick of time."

It took above two hours to make everything satisfactory between the burly captain and Don Mariano, but this we eventually did.

A MOOR.

"Now," said the great-hearted captain, "come right aboard my ship, and I 'll take you fellows home. You 've been drifting about long enough, have n't you? Come aboard, anyway, and stay while I 'm here. Yes, you must. I won't take no for an answer. Where 's your dunnage, anyway?"

As the captain would not "take no for an answer," we all gladly went aboard his ship, — a fine large barque at anchor in the bay. To our great joy we found that our new friend was bound for Algeria, for a port in Eastern Algiers known as Oran. The next day we were well under way along the African coast, speeding eastward.

A desire to get a glimpse of that portion of Africa whence Spain, in ancient times, had been invaded by fierce hordes that became civilized and rose to eminence under the genial clime of their adopted country, had taken us to Morocco. Now we were to leave it with hardly more than a hint of its treasures of antiquity. But the world is large; only the stay-at-home, absorbed in his garden or shop, is

FEATS OF HORSEMANSHIP AT THE FÊTE OF MAHOMET.

supremely satisfied with his surroundings. That he is right, I do not doubt. Blessed be the man whose aspirations are bounded by his farm or the four walls of his home; thrice blessed he who has wife and little ones to share his lot! But when a man has neither home nor family, why should he not turn himself loose upon the world? It cannot satisfy, but it can give him food for thought, — the wherewithal to fill unpleasant hours.

That home is the place for man, I do not doubt. Ever before him rises the mirage of a home, of a haven of rest, where his old age at least may be spent, and where he may gather about him the circle of his friends. But it is an *ignis fatuus*, it always keeps just ahead; he cannot rest; the world, like a vigilant patrol, says to him, "Move on; this is no place for you."

In vain the traveller expostulates: "It was not of my asking; had I my choice, I would be tilling soil to-day." But the world is inexorable: "Move on, or off the stage." And so he goes, ever before him visions of a resting-place, until the friends he fain would have gathered round him are dead or estranged, and he halts not until he stumbles into his grave.

But, pardon; we did not intend to digress. Let us to our voyage.

Late one afternoon we arrived opposite the sad and lonely settlement of Melilla, a frontier post in possession of the Spanish; their only hold (I think, save Ceuta) upon any portion of Africa. Their once powerful settlements upon the African coast have dwindled to these pitiful towns, half of which are composed of forts and prisons. But the old fortifications are picturesque, overhanging the sea with gray, time-buffeted walls. Beyond again, on an island, is a penal settlement, likewise Spanish, but at some distance from the coast.

Another morning, after quiet sailing, we arrived off Nemours, the westernmost port in the possession of the French in Africa. Fine views are afforded of the hills beyond, but the port itself is wretched, and the town consists apparently of a single street along the shore, hemmed in and frowned upon by barren hills. There is no sheltered harbor, and landing is precariously made in clumsy boats. Two immense rocks, called The Brothers, stand isolated at the entrance to the bay. Later on, we arrived opposite the harbor we were anxious to enter, just as the sun was setting, and the dusk enveloping all in haze.

We sailed in from the Caribbean, and past the headlands crowned by ancient forts. I cannot forget, as I look upon these fort-crowned hills, dim in the obscurity of night, that here was the first of the Spanish conquests that eventually extended Spanish power over Algiers, Tunis, and Tripoli. Cardinal Ximenes, in his famous expedition, commanded by Navarro, the skilled engineer of the Italian campaigns, captured these forts, slew four thousand Moors, and took great stores of plunder. It was such a holy war, and the chroniclers were so put to it for adequate description, that they gravely relate that the *sun stood still* until the Cardinal gained his victory!

As the scenery, the immediate surroundings, of Oran and its history are interdependent, let us first glance at the latter, merely to assure ourselves that it has a history. About a thousand years ago, or, to be exact, in the year 902, two Moorish merchants from Spain came over here and stationed themselves for the purposes of trade. As there was (and is) a deep ravine, leading down to the sea, they gave their location the Arabic appellation *Wahran*, the Ravine. From this name comes Oran, by which it has been known in all modern times. The ancient pronunciation, however, still clings to the name, and Wahran it is called to this day. Its first civilized settlers were driven out in the year 909, and little more is known of it till about the middle of the twelfth century, when it was possessed by the Almoahides. After their overthrow, about the middle of the thirteenth century, Oran was annexed to the kingdom of Tlemcen, becoming the port of that beautiful capital in the desert, — that city of the saints and last resort of the Moors.

About the time America was discovered (as we all know, or ought to know), the last stronghold of the Moors was taken from them, and the people, expelled from Spain, from Granada and the fertile vegas of Andalusia, flocked to Africa by thousands and

NEMOURS.

tens of thousands. Many went to Morocco, doubtless landing at Tangier, but most of them came to Oran, settling here, and spreading hence over the interior of the country, and chiefly about Tlemcen. The last king of Granada, the unfortunate Moular-Ben-Hassan, fled hither when driven from the Alhambra and the last of his castles in Andalusia. About 1500, when the implacable Ferdinand the Catholic had wiped out the last vestige of Moorish possession in Spain, Wahran became quite a resort for pirates and corsairs, who deemed (and not without reason) the commerce of the so-called Christians a legitimate subject of prey.

In the year 1505, the great (if not good) Cardinal Ximenes, not content with the extirpation of the Moors in Spain, and the burning and massacring of thousands of heretics by means of the holy Inquisition, persuaded Ferdinand to allow him to equip a force and a squadron for the subjugation of Oran. With the vigor characteristic of this great bigot, Ximenes supplied the funds for an expedition, under command of Diego de Cordova. This force succeeded in capturing the strong fortress of Mars-el-Kebir, and four years later the great Cardinal himself led another expedition, which captured Oran, and the mountain fortress that dominated the port. As all those who fought in this holy war were granted indulgence from fast-days all the rest of their lives, the Cardinal did not lack for soldiers, many of whom needed no more indulgences on this earth, and doubtless soon found out the road to heaven, or hell, without the aid of the monk; for the fortress was situated on a height impregnable, and they took it only after desperate fighting, and after covering the hillside with the slain. The successful Spaniards now had the pleasure of reducing the last Moorish stronghold to subjection, and of murdering many more thousands through the medium of the iniquitous Inquisition.

The Spaniards gained no more than this, besides the treasure of the city, and the conversion of the mosques into churches.

Barbarossa the corsair, King of Algiers, attempted to capture Oran from the Spaniards in 1509, but was defeated with great slaughter. It was not until two centuries later, in 1708, that the Turks succeeded in wresting Oran from the Spaniards. In 1732, the year that George Washington was born, the Spaniards celebrated this great event by once more taking town and castles from the followers of Mahomet. What they wanted it for, nobody knows; but about that time the Spaniards were prone to take anything they could lay their hands on. They held Oran for sixty years, but in 1790 the Turks, aided by an earthquake that nearly destroyed town and fortress, forced the Spaniards to capitulate. A treaty was concluded in 1791, and in 1792 the Spaniards left the territory, and have not returned since, except that thousands now come over annually from that poverty-stricken country across the Straits in search of labor and the means of sustenance. They form a very considerable part of the population, poorer even than the Arabs, dirtier than the French, and in some respects meaner than the Jews. For about forty years Oran was governed, or misgoverned, by the Beys of Algiers, until in 1830 the coming of the French dispossessed the last of that murderous brood, since which time the city has enjoyed a measure of peace, if not of prosperity.

As to the attractions of Oran to the stranger, a great deal may depend upon the stranger. No part of the Mediterranean, perhaps, can exceed it in picturesqueness of environment. The town itself is built upon the steep northern slope of the hill Murdjadjo, the great ravine Wahran almost bisecting its upper portion, but filled in toward the sea, and covered with buildings. A thousand feet above the town rises the hill, crowned by the port of Santa Cruz; a little before it stands a Gothic chapel, crowned by a colossal statue of Nôtre Dame de la salud de Santa Cruz, said to be a replica of the Virgin of Nôtre Dame de la Garde, at Marseilles. The white figure, with its hands extended in perpetual benediction, seems to extend its blessing to those who had performed the devout work of suppressing here the religion of Mahomet. But, as if to mock this endeavor of the Christians to commemorate the achievements of the followers of the cross, the Arabs have erected a tomb to their patron saint of Oran, Sidi-Kebir, on the crest of the ridge, several hundred feet above; the white dome of this *marabout* is visible farther than the marble figure of the Virgin; and in the town beneath, the great mosque of the Moors is as vigorously protected by the government as the cathedral of the Catholics.

One evening, an hour before sunset, I climbed the steep road that leads to the fortress of San Gregoin, a few hundred feet below the chapel, and then clambered over the steeps to the chapel and fort above. The ascent was so sharp that I could hardly maintain a foothold; yet up this mountain, more than once, had mail-clad soldiers dashed to the charge. I finally reached the fort, only to find the entrance barred, the structure deserted. It rose above me stern and frowning, without a projecting scarp or abutment by which one might lay hold and climb to its parapet; yet this same fortress had been twice taken by assault, — how, no one can now conceive. The only approach to it at all is along a knife-like crest which one might sit astride, and even then there seems but slight hold for scaling-ladders to be placed. How many must have perished ere the strong walls were taken; every crimson rock must have been drenched in blood, and the entire crest covered with the corpses of the slain. Beyond, across a deep gap in the ridge, there is a table-topped hill even higher, where, on the edge of the precipice, is the white tomb of Sidi-Kebir. From this point the fort could be bombarded, as it dominates it, and doubtless the troops of Ximenes brought cannon here and first opened a breach in the walls before they pressed on to carry it by assault.

The view from chapel, fort, or tomb is most magnificent. To the north the far-sweeping horizon line of the Mediterranean, east, the harbor, and beyond, a yellow coast crowned by the distant mountain of Kristel; from the base of the hill stretches the town, with creamy walls and roofs of sunburnt tiles, its surface broken by dome and minarets and the towers of church and cathedral. At least eight forts, including the two on the hill, can be seen; they guard every strategic point and thrust out their massive walls from every hill and angle of the wall. For this city is still surrounded by walls, with bastions and gates, and is guarded as in the time of the Turks and Moors.

Beneath and toward the west is Mars-el-Kebir, where a projecting promontory, some four miles from Oran, shelters a beautiful bay and quiet village. The point is strongly fortified. The fort of El Kebir, said to cover the site of one previously erected by the Romans, has undergone as many vicissitudes as that above Oran. It was taken by Cordova in 1505; in 1708 the Turks retook it and massacred its entire garrison, three hundred in number; they lost it again in 1732, and again captured it in 1791, the last conquest being by the French. Reminiscences of Spanish occupation are found here in the shape of the arms of Ferdinand over the fountain at the entrance, and on the shore of the bay toward Oran in some warm mineral baths known as Les Bains de la Reine, from the visit of Isabella early in the sixteenth century, with her infant daughter. An excellent road leads around the coast in this direction, leaving the fort beneath high cliffs, passing through a short tunnel, and all the way giving far-reaching views of the sea.

The ravine and steep escarpment of the hill toward the town are thickly planted with pines so as to form a dense forest, in refreshing contrast to the denuded rocks around. Some of the trees are a foot in diameter, and all are carefully tended under the oversight of the same wise Frenchmen who are looking to the future reclamation of these barren hillsides. By this means they have entirely changed the aspect of the scenery, and added a new element

FÊTE AT THE ANNIVERSARY OF THE BIRTH OF MAHOMET.

of beauty to the scene as one views it from the town or public garden. Although the hills seem barren, yet they are covered, as are the plains, with flowers of every hue, that spread out sheets of color here, and nestle in sheltered places there, growing out of crevices in the rocks, and in the nooks and crannies of the fort. Perhaps the best place whence to view the castle-crowned hill is from the terrace or garden rising above the port, and planted everywhere with shrubs and flowers. Winding walks lead all about, and through the branches of pines and date-palms gleams the red hillside with its yellow-walled forts. Some of the terraces are covered with a small vine bearing thick mats of flowers, and are perfect sheets of purple bloom. Here also you look down upon the enclosed harbor, the scene of busy maritime life, where there are sometimes a dozen steamers moored, and where a thick cluster of lateen-rigged vessels occupy the inner quarter of the mole. Railway tracks lead out to the main station, a mile beyond, and thence run to Algiers, to Tunis, and far into the border-land of the Great Desert. This port of Oran is at a time not far distant destined to be the great entrepot for an immense commerce with the vast interior of Africa, of the Soudan perhaps, certainly of Morocco.

Crowning the hill whose slopes the gardens cover, rise the vast fortifications of the Kasba, where once the Bey resided, which dates from a time anterior to the Spanish conquest, and which was surrendered to the great Ximenes Cisueros. The walls rise forty, fifty, in places perhaps one hundred feet, above the roadway; they throw out buttresses, project ornate sentry-boxes, upon the steep ravines as well as directly upon the most thickly settled portion of the city. In fact, one can hardly turn a corner without coming upon a fortress wall, a stone tower, or some vestige of a demolished castle. Many of the houses are built into and out of these ancient walls; the city is full of ruins, and the suburbs are seamed with the lines of former military constructions. The scars of sieges and earthquakes are mostly covered with plasters of vegetation, as every available plot of earth supports a garden, overrunning with vines, fig-trees, and flowering plants. Here innumerable humble habitations nestle on the slopes of the ravines, where their residents cultivate assiduously the little garden spots, rich in vegetables of every kind, and without the sign of a weed within their precincts.

An interesting place in the great ravine is the immense covered establishment with open sides where the washerwomen of the city meet in great numbers. Water is free to all for the taking, and flows through the streets as well as through the irrigated fields and gardens. The pleasantest spot of all is the garden above the Place République, where one may sit in shade or sun, beneath the pines, and look down upon the busy life below. Steamers come and go, one for Marseilles, another for Algiers, another for Malaga, all within short gunshot of your garden-seat.

The sun wheels slowly round and falls behind the western hill, lighting up the yellow coast and the dun hills beyond with mist-gathering hollows and darkening slopes; the triangular sails of the fishing-boats gleam white against the blue; it quickly grows dusk and cool, the sound of labor ceases below, and the noise of travel comes only from the streets and promenades around the squares. Birds of bright plumage chirp among the trees; a great mass of purple-blossomed vines sends out heavy yet delicious odors; the lower walls of the Kasba are in gloom, the upper only bright in the last rays of the sun as it sinks finally behind the sharp crest of the *cerro*. It is dawn now, and the coolness of evening quickly causes one to retire from his seat beneath the pines.

Of antiquities, Oran can boast little if anything antedating the Arab invasion; but in its museum is shown a well-arranged collection of marbles and mosaics, mainly obtained from towns to the north. These are all Roman, and are but a few of the many remains of that people found scattered along the northern coast of

Africa. Some of these mosaics cover a surface fifteen feet square, and are of very excellent workmanship. A description of them has been printed by the Society of Oran, and gives us an insight into a civilization of nearly fifteen centuries ago. Like the French, the Romans were good road-builders, and wherever they penetrated into Africa they left monuments of their work in the shape of roads, mile-stones, and aqueducts.

I might mention a score of towns, modern French and Arab settlements, built on the sites of ancient Roman towns. I have mentioned the mosque. Its minaret, detached from the main structure, is a conspicuous object in the centre of the town, and is beautifully ornamented with borders of tiles. The main entrance of the mosque is handsome, but is a restoration by a French artist, and lacks the charm of antiquity. All the mosques in Algiers are open to strangers on the simple condition that they take off their shoes, while the mosques of Morocco cannot be entered by a Christian unbeliever. In Oran, the Mahometans are most liberal, not even asking the stranger to remove his shoes, but giving him a pair of clogs into which he slips his feet and goes clattering over the floor.

CHAPTER VI.

A RAILROAD JOURNEY IN ALGIERS.

F anything be needed to illustrate French push and progress, and the fitness of the French, after the Gauls, for successful colonizers, it is to be found in their manner of road and railway construction. The French are the Romans of to-day, in the way of road-making. From every seaport, from every important city, roads and railways ramify in every direction, and are all trending toward the great and mysterious interior region known as the Desert. But as they push farther and farther southward, the Great Desert vanishes before them, and is only heard when the locust clouds come up, and the scorching siroccos sweep along the plains. More than a thousand miles of railroad are now built in Algiers, or rather along the north coast of Africa. The various lines operate under different names, but all combine to form one vast system; so that the traveller can enter Africa at Oran and journey clear to Tunis without breaking his journey oftener than he would desire for rest. And these roads are well built, stone ballasted, with massive viaducts and gentle gradients; though the rolling stock consists of those hideous and abominable cars and wagons we see in France and Spain. The distance from Oran to Algiers (city) is 421 kilometers, and the first-class fare is 48 francs; from Algiers to Constantine, 464 kilometers; from Constantine (or Kroubs) to Tunis, 450 kilometers, the whole dis-

tance being 1335 kilometers, or about 850 miles. The various branch lines are constantly extending, creeping nearer and nearer the Desert country, so that no exact figures can be given; but they will aggregate at least one hundred and fifty miles, making a full thousand constructed up to 1889. These branches extend from near Oran to Hemen, and to Mascara; from Philipville and Constantine to Batna, El Kantara, and Biskra; and one is projected from the Port of Bone and the main line to the Gulf of Cabes.

Nowhere in the world, does it seem to me, is there such a magnificent opportunity for development and civilization as in Africa, and especially that portion now controlled by the French. The French, as colonizers, are better than the English to deal with barbarous peoples. Before the Anglo-Saxons, barbarians and semi-civilized peoples melt away like snow before the sun. With the French, however, the case is different. They never exterminate, but *assimilate*. They certainly have very tough subjects in the stern and sullen Arabs, who hold themselves aloof, in lofty scorn of the Europeans; but they have made some advance with the city-dwelling Moors, and even with the Jews and the Berbers. Negroes and Indians are the chosen peoples with whom the French readily amalgamate, choosing their dusky partners with greater regard to their sympathetic qualities than their beauty. The resultant race, or sub-race, is certainly an improvement upon the original (barbarous) stock, as instance the mulattoes and octaroons of the West Indies, and the Canadian half-castes. But the nomadic Arab: the Frenchman glances at him askance; and as the follower of Mahomet has no attractive harem or fraction of a harem for the Frenchman's entertainment, the Gaul turns to and mauls him into submission.

The French have moved along several lines of progression and conquest. They have steadily advanced, and held everything they have gained.

Saying good-by to our noble friend the Captain, we started out from Oran on the early morning train, expecting to arrive at Algiers, the capital of Algeria, that night. We found the train crowded with excursionists, for the scientific men of all France had crowded down here to attend a meeting at Oran. They were true excursionists, nevertheless, and all eager to get their money's worth as they went along.

TRAVELLING IN ALGERIA.

At Affreville, where we halted for dinner, there was such a rush for the station as would have disgraced the worst and hungriest crowd in America. It resembled such a scramble as Dickens described when he drew upon his vivid imagination to adorn the facts. The few women in the crowd were last in the whirl of mad and excited Gauls who fought for seats in the dining-hall. That they did not get trampled upon and their lives jammed out of them was owing to the fact that they were Frenchwomen, and knew what brutes their lords and masters were; hence they fought shy of the crowd and waited, picking up such crumbs as the hogs had left.

The infrequent towns along the line, as they are generally at a distance from the railroad, much resemble each other, and hardly any one is of conspicuous interest, save for its history. Most of these towns are of recent growth, dating from since the French invasion. The remains of the Arabs consist chiefly of the *Koubbas*, or tombs of saints, which gleam white on the hill-crests, or adorn some swelling elevation of the plain.

The history of this section refers us to the French, but beyond the French are the Arabs. "We shall not easily forget," says a recent writer, "the splendid comet of Arab civilization that has left such a trail of light behind it, but cannot help remarking that neither the Arab in a state of nature, nor the Moor surrounded by every refinement of luxury, seems to be influenced by the grace and beauty around him. And in this they do not stand alone; for it is a notable fact that mere *contact with what is beautiful in scenery or art* is of itself of little worth. Nor does it lead to cleanliness, or godliness, or any other virtue. In Algiers we see the great tides of civilization, primitive and modern,— the East and the West,— meet and mingle without limit and without confusion. The industries of the Moors are of the Middle Ages. They still have ancient looms, and still make the wonderful Saracenic locks, with their ponderous keys." Another writer notes that the Bedouins of the town are very different from the Nomads, who are tall and frank, with bronze complexion and long, quick stride. The equipment of a Berber, or Bedouin, consists of a long old percussion musket, two old pistols, and a yataghan, or Bedouin sword. The Arab woman, he says, has the same treatment as twelve hundred years ago. She is neither wife, mistress, nor companion. The women prepare that peculiar food called the *kuss-kuss* from the wheat, and in its preparation are said to squirt water over it from their mouths.

The Arab horseman wears but one spur, it is said, because he reasons that when one side of the horse is spurred the other *must* run.

One thing I noted in Algiers,—that everybody there drank what he liked; even the children imbibed *ad lib.* There was but one prerequisite, and that was that the child should at least be as big as the bottle.

Among the scientific men I met on my journey was the well-known geographer Elisie Réclus, who speaks English with fluency, having lived in New Orleans. Now and then our conversation would remind me of my French landlady in the West Indies. She was an English student, and to show her proficiency would frequently write me little notes, as for instance: "Do write everything which you will," and "He is alone now, but when you go more he happy to come with you."

MOSQUE OF SIDI ABD-ER-RAHHMANN.

We kept on until late in the afternoon, and then the country was blotted out by the sinking of the sun.

The distance from Oran to Algiers was 421 kilometers, or about two hundred miles, and we covered the distance with little fatigue, and saw much of interest by the way. During the journey, in the

AN ALGERIAN BEAUTY

monotonous places, the Doctor beguiled the hours away by telling stories, and one of these, about a certain doubtful character he once met in the West Indies, we repeat here. Let him tell it in his own words: —

MR. HOOPER AND HIS OLLAPOD.

My acquaintance with Mr. Thomas Hooper began on a slow-going steamer bound for Cuba and Mexico. It was in the exciting times of the first railway ventures. Every steamer going Mexico-ward was loaded to the full with engineers from every part of the world, — England, Germany, and South America, — but a large majority fresh from the schools of the United States. They were just starting out in life, and most of them were well endowed with funds, furnished by fond parents and relatives who were anxious they should carve out for themselves great careers in a foreign land. I do not consider it irrelevant to remark that I met the last one of them four years later, and he was inquiring of his fellow-Americans for money enough to pay his passage back to the States. All of them had failed in the carving of careers.

Mr. Hooper, as I intended to say, was passenger on our steamer. He was not an engineer, in the strictest sense of the word, nor merely a pleasure tourist. No one, indeed, knew why he was going to Mexico, though it was finally surmised that he was interested in mines, and this surmise became something more, until it was at last told as a positive fact that Mr. Hooper was owner of "vast deposits of the precious metal" somewhere in the interior of Mexico. To such as inquired of him as to the truth of these rumors, he would wink confidentially, and intimate that he knew a thing or two more than rumor did; then he would invariably order duplicate cocktails for two, and, the while they disappeared, gradually impart the details of a mining scheme that would set his hearer wild with a desire to be a participant in its risks and profits. Half our company had lost their senses — and a few of them something more substantial — over Hooper's glorious scheme before we had reached Havana, only four days out from New York. The strangest thing about it was, that no one seemed to know Hooper when he came aboard, and all our information of that individual had been acquired from that individual himself. Yet the impression had crept abroad that he was not only very wealthy, but that he possessed that Midas touch which converted all' he handled into golden treasure. Personally, he was not particularly attractive; his hair had the unassuming hue of an unburnt brick, his nose was rendered hopelessly obscure by blotches of freckles, while his eyes, where they were not yellow, were apparently as freckled as his nose. But he was good-natured all the day long, and the feats he performed with his firearms were so wonderful as to excite the admiration of all beholders. It was a favorite pastime with him to knock a "nickel" off the rail from across the deck; and this was invariably accomplished every morning, whether the steamer was gliding smoothly along or pitching wildly about in the short waves of the gulf.

And his good humor was only equalled by his *sang froid;* for you might wake him out of a sound sleep at any time of night and he would open his eyes as bright as a dollar, and drawl out in his peculiar tone, "I know you're wrong, but I'm wid ye; drive on with the corpse!" He was lying asleep under the rail one day, when it occurred to a passenger that it would be a fine thing to tickle his ear with a straw. He lay on his back, with his mouth open to the sky; a fly crawling on his nose made no impression on him; he was evidently fast asleep. One hand was in the pocket of his blouse, the other hung toward the deck. As the passenger approached with his straw, an eager crowd gathered about to see the fun. "Bet five dollars he'll tickle him off the bench," whispered one of the group, as the straw approached his ear. There was a muffled click in the pocket that held the hand, and some one cried out, "Take care! he's going to shoot!" As the crowd dispersed, the voice of Hooper drawled out: "I'll take that V, if you please." He claimed the bet and got it, and his person was thenceforward as sacred as that of the Grand Lama.

It was a day or two before we landed at Vera Cruz that whispers were interchanged regarding the mysterious character of an invention of Hooper's which but a few of the passengers had investigated, — the Ollapod. Even those who were thought to have seen it preserved the secret so well that nothing material was elicited by all our questioning; but it was noticed that a certain number of the male passengers — generally those who were most expert players of poker and other national games — retired to the captain's cabin late in the evening, whence some of them had been seen to emerge the following morning by such of our company as rose early in order to see the sun rise and the decks washed. But most of us landed at the "ancient city" little the wiser regarding the Ollapod. Two of our company, — two young engineers, — who started out fullest of confidence and cash, lingered behind as the rest of us were rowed to the mole, and it was given out that they were "strapped" and obliged to return to New York in the same steamer that brought them out. They were observed to cast black looks at the smiling Hooper as he bade them adieu with his customary effusion of speech, and one of them — his name was Cooney — cursed him to his face, and swore

AN ALGERIAN ANTELOPE-HUNTER.

he would expose the Ollapod to the New York police. "All right," said Hooper, cheerfully, "you can say you 've seen it; but," lowering his voice ominously, "you 'll have to admit that you had a hand at the game."

The reception that was given Hooper by the American residents of Mexico, upon his arrival at the capital, was in truth an ovation. It was told afterward that the carriages, the musicos, and the enthusiastic brethren that went down to welcome him, were paid for doing so out of Hooper's own pocket. But he silenced the dissatisfied by giving a select spread at the Café Concordia, at which he explained to us several new schemes on hand by which he would extract tons and tons of precious metal from the bowels of mother earth; and the Mexican papers contained full accounts of the enthusiastic reception accorded the generous young Americano, el Señor Don Tomaso Hoopero, who had come down to Mexico to expend millions of dollars in exploring its undeveloped resources. His mines, they understood, were already in bonanza, and a company was being formed for the further working of them. "Fortunate, indeed, the individual who could secure shares in the company of Don Tomaso!"

To the Mexican editor the unfound and consequently undeveloped resources of Mexico are vast, beyond the comprehension of man; they are destined to enrich millions! But no Mexican in recent years has ever attempted to find them, save through the aid of foreign capital.

But the working of mines — on paper — did not comprise all the strings to Don Tomaso's bow. About that time vague reports crept out anent the great "Anglo-Americano-Mexicano lottery of Kentucky," of which Don Tomaso was agent. Certain young men, friends of his, were displaying more money than had been their wont, and it did not take long for the public to trace the silver stream to its source. Groups of excited Mexicans gathered on the corners as Don Tomaso passed, and he was pointed out by everybody in the plaza. He was then in the zenith of his glory, and his costume was ultra Mexican, — sombrero big as an Englishman's tub and loaded with shining silver, leather jacket richly embroidered, pantaloons decked with rows of silver buttons, heels armed with enormous spurs that clanked threateningly as he strode along, while his revolver was the biggest and shiniest of the hundreds that depended from the belts of gorgeous caballeros. And as his reputation as a dead shot had been spread abroad, he received the most deferential treatment from the Mexicanos, who carry their shooting-irons more for ornament than use.

Don Tomaso had no regular office, as the law prohibited a foreign lottery from absorbing the cash of residents, it being needed for home affairs of similar description. But his room at the hotel was filled with young men night and day, chiefly Mexicans of good families, wide-awake, eager-looking fellows, who regarded Hooper as an exceedingly valuable acquaintance, and who confided to his care hundreds of pesos for investment in the A.-A.-Mexicano. For it was a curious feature of the workings of this lottery, that nearly every ticket drew a prize; that is, every one Hooper had sold on his previous visit, the money for which, awarded at the last grand drawing, he had now brought with him. Nearly every American you met would corner you and ask excitedly if you had invested in Hooper's latest scheme, at the same time telling of his good luck in drawing a prize of fifty dollars or one hundred dollars. A few Mexicans had also been equally fortunate; and they and their friends trooped to his room by dozens, all eager to invest their last real, and sanguine that at last they had found a lottery conducted with a due regard for the interests of the investor. During the month of his stay Hooper managed to gather to himself most of the loose silver of his friends, and then set out again for the "States," leaving every one of them confident that his ticket would draw the grand prize of ten thousand dollars. So thoroughly were they convinced of this, that they combined their scanty leavings and gave him a grand banquet on the evening preceding his departure, which manifestation of confidence was duly reported in the morning papers, and placed on file by the sagacious Don Tomaso for future use. Some unforeseen accident must have delayed the "grand distribution," for Hooper never returned to disburse; at least, I found some of his investors waiting for him three years afterward.

It was two years after the Mexican episode that I again met Señor Hooper, in a broker's office on Broadway, at the time when excitement over the Grant and Ward affair was at white heat. He was then stopping at a hotel on Fifth Avenue, to mention which would betray Hooper at once, for he was known to everybody there, from bell-boy to proprietor. He had married since our last meeting, and nothing would do but I must post up with him and see his wife. Then I learned that he had just returned from South America, and was on the eve of departure for Africa. When questioned, he reluctantly admitted that he had been, and was going, in the interests of an English syndicate in the rubber business; that he had spotted all the likely places along the Amazon and the Congo, and was going out to secure the last stick of caoutchouc for the syndicate. With still greater reluctance he "allowed" that he had taken the Ollapod along with him, and that the South Americans had derived great benefit from the workings, having read the notices of his grand reception in the Mexican papers.

"And now we're going to the Congo, me and Virginny here, and if you'll just go along, we'll make an everlasting fortune. Wha-at? Yes, we'll take the Ollapod, and you can write an account of the trip, and we'll sell the Ollapod and book together. Fact, every native will want an Ollapod, and book thrown in, for five dollars; that's the price, — five dollars for small size, twenty-five dollars for a big one. What is the Ollapod? Wha-at? Ain't you seen one yet? Wa-al if our'n wa'n't all packed I'd tell you in about a minute. It's just the darndest contrivance you ever did see! Big as a clock? Yes, some of 'em is, and some is n't. You see, I have 'em to suit all complexions; some of 'em 's the size of a watch, and some ain't. Describe it? Certainly, jest as lives as not. In the first place, it's a board, painted off in different colors, chiefly red and black; then it has a representation of everything you want to know; for instance, there's the world, painted out large as life, and inside the circle is the diameter of the globe, distance from the sun, *et cetery*, and so forth, then there's the sun, hits diameter and circumference; then there's all the biggest cities on the globe, — London, four million population; New York, fifteen hundred thousand population, went Democratic last 'lection, etc. In fact, there ain't anything you want to know that ain't there. What's the use of it? Why, it's better 'n a g'ography, a plum sight; and then, again, I sometimes use it to kill time with. You see, there's a neat arrangement, so that if you roll a ball — which goes with the Ollapod — in a certain direction it's sure to strike the earth, or the sun, or the largest city, etc. And the man that bets on the sun, why, he takes the pot; and, — well, now, you see how 't is yourself; they generally buck agin the table, — that's me, and — they generally git left! Them Mexican fellers? Oh, yes; you see they nearly always bet on the sun, and then the board would happen to be canted toward the moon, and *vice versy*. Policemen ever seen it? Bless your soul, yes, sir, heaps of times; but what right have they to interfere in a historico-geographical game like the Ollapod? No right at all. Yes, sir; I'm going up the Congo after rubber, and I shall take the Ollapod along to give the niggers a lesson in g'ography."

The Professor, who is nothing if not practical or statistical, then gave us some information about the country we were travelling in, — Algeria. It extends along the coast about five hundred and fifty miles, and stretches inland three hundred and fifty miles and more, lying between 2° 10′ west and 8° 50′ east longitude, and 32° to 37° north latitude. It is divided into two distinct regions, — the

Tell and the Sahara; the former the land of corn, and fertile, the latter the desert country. The Sahara is divided into mountainous, sandy, and oasis regions, the coldest month being January and the hottest August. The railroad line runs a great distance through the *Metidja*, — the plain of great fertility that lies between the Atlas foot-hills and the Sahel. Tall eucalyptus-trees at times line the track and are seen in many groves.

MOSQUE OF SIDI SALAHH, AT OUARGLA.

Tree-planting on a vast scale has been undertaken here in Algiers, and with the most beneficial results. Where formerly was sun-scorched desert, a sterile hillside, a damp miasmatic swamp-land, the beneficent eucalypti spread their limbs, filling the air with balsamic odors in place of miasm, and giving shade and fertility, in conjunction with judicious drainage and artesian wells. The town of Boufarik is an example of what European energy can accomplish in Africa, with its stream-bordered streets, shaded avenues and squares, where was once a swamp so malarious that the first settlers died like sheep. The native trees of value here in Algiers are the cork-tree, cedar, ilex, aleppo, and maritime pine, the olive, fig, citrus family, and palms. But of all trees, the Australian gum-

AN OASIS OF THE ALGERIAN SAHARA.

trees, the eucalypti, are the most valuable in the *reboisement* of Algiers. That it is the determined purpose of the French to re-forest this north coast of Africa is a fact that commands the approbation of the world.

The Metidja is estimated to contain five hundred thousand acres of land, one half of which is susceptible of being cultivated with success, by the aid of irrigation, by means of artesian wells and *barrages*, or reservoirs. The cereals flourish here, but in small fruits and vegetables Algeria excels. Figs, oranges, olives, and especially grapes find here a favorable soil and climate. The figs prefer the mountain-sides and hills, the oranges the coast; the vineyards, the hope of the country, are chiefly on the seaside hills. The date — that fruit and salvation of the desert — is not found in its perfection along the coast.

But I must not let these side glimpses of African agriculture divert us from the beaten track. The fact is, though, that the possibilities of Algeria seem to me so great, — guarding as it does the avenue of approach to the mysterious continent, — that I am constantly forced into speculation upon its resources, and the fate of the people engaged in working out the problem of the re-conquest of Africa by Europeans. The French have gone about it in an intelligent way. They mean to create here a New France, and I think they will succeed. It is now fifty-eight years since they landed their troops here, and they have had time at least to declare their intentions, if not to effect a conquest of the native tribes and the forces of Nature.

I, for one, am thankful that the French came into Africa, and hope they will extend their roads and railways until the Great Desert is crossed, and we can reach Senegal and the mysterious Beyond.

In due time we reached Algiers; but before we proceed to describe that capital of Algeria, allow me to describe a side-journey we took to the sacred tombs of Blidah and the holy city of Tlemcen.

CHAPTER VII.

ARAB TOMBS AND ARAB CITIES.

 PASSPORT is not necessary in Algiers; but you are required at the hotels to give those little items of information about yourself that the police prize so highly. Then, you are free to go and come at your leisure. Of the various excursions in the neighborhood of the city, that to Blidah and the gorge of Chiffa is the most often recommended. At the former place is wild and rugged scenery, great rocks, and running streams, and troops of wild monkeys that sometimes show themselves to tourists. The trip to Blidah I took on my way to Oran; as to its attractions, let the following lines be placed in testimony. The railway service here, though European, is tolerably good; the trains depart and arrive on time, and there are rarely any accidents of note. The line first skirts the beautiful bay, and then, at ten kilometers distance from the city, turns to the southwest and enters the Metidja.

In due season we reached Blidah, a town of eight thousand inhabitants, fifty kilometers from Algiers. It lies at the base of the Atlas range, with the Metidja spread below to the Sahel beyond. An omnibus carried me to the Hôtel Geronde, where I found a neat room, a cool inner court overhung with vines, and meals with excellent service. One good thing the French have done, — they have carried everywhere, into every village and hamlet, their excellent cuisine; their neatness and thrift always commend them to the tired and thirsty traveller.

It did not take me long to see the town, for its attractions are few, though unique, and after lunch I sallied forth with my camera. The inevitable Arab went along with me, and conducted me first to the sacred grove of olive-trees.

Though there are many groves and gardens here, the finest is the *Bois Sacré*,—the sacred grove of olives,—in the suburbs of the town. They are sacred because they contain and shelter the *koubbas*, or mosque-like tombs of some holy *marabouts*, or Arab saints. They are indeed beautiful, these white and marble-like structures with domed roofs, and the giant olives, hung with trailing mosses, rise above and enclose them in a twilight-gloom that is conducive to thoughts of worship. Now and then the sun strikes through the canopy of foliage, and draws a tracery of leaf and limb upon the marbled surface of the tombs, painting these fleeting pictures all day long. Silent Arabs glide stealthily away, emerging from the gloom, pausing a moment to pray, perhaps, then disappearing again without a sound.

I tried in vain to induce some of these Arabs, hooded in their white *burnouses*, to pose at the tomb a moment; they all indignantly refused. At last my guide consented to don a *burnous* and sit upon an olive-stump in a devotional attitude, while I secured his image with my camera.

These *koubbas*, though so delightfully situated, are not the holiest of Blidah, for there are others above, up the ravine, that exceed them in sanctity. With my guide, I walked along the river-bank some two miles, up a gorge that seemed to penetrate to the heart of Atlas. There we found an Arab cemetery, with many quaint headstones, and two large tombs held in peculiar veneration. The oldest is over three hundred years old, and covers the remains of Sidi Ahmed el Kebir, a *marabout* of great sanctity.

More attractive to me than the tombs were the cavalry barracks, where is the finest stud of Arabian stallions (it is said) in the world. Permission was given me to view these magnificent animals, and a soldier went the rounds with me, while my guide was obliged to remain at the gate. My soldier-guide was polite and attentive, but did not disdain the silver I offered him; in truth, it slipped into his pocket in a way that seemed to suggest the filling of a long-felt want.

THE MOORISH METHOD OF PLOUGHING.

Blidah, though pleasant enough, with its orange-groves and running streams, could not detain me more than a night, for there was a city in the desert toward which my journey trended.

Nobody seemed to know where Tlemcen was, when I made inquiry at Oran, but at last I was told to go to Ain Temouchent by rail, and there take diligence. This I did, reaching Ain Temouchent about dusk. I then found that a diligence started at midnight and another early in the morning. Finding a little *posada*, or inn, here, kept by a jolly old Frenchman, who was delighted to find that I came from America and that I spoke Spanish, I engaged a room and meals. The morning diligence started on time, and I started with it, having a seat beside the driver, which commanded views of the surrounding country. Of the first half of our journey I remember little more than that the roads were excellent and the scenery uninteresting. To maintain this highway to Tlemcen in perfect state, the road-menders are stationed at intervals, who fill the ruts with broken rock, and lay out long beds of this material, which the diligence is obliged to drive over because large rocks are laid across the smooth portion of the road. Our course, consequently, was a very sinuous one, as the driver had to veer from side to side to avoid the lines of rocks. Now and then we ran over a rock, receiving thereby a great jolt, and extorting a volley of curses from the inside passengers. Our driver, a short, sturdy Gaul in blue cotton blouse, was the hardest-worked man I saw in Algiers, for he was constantly lashing our mules, and shouting at them.

The first distinct image I had of an approach to the desert region was of a group of Arab tents and a drove of camels. The camels were ranging the barren pasture-land, and seemed as much at home as cows in a field of clover. I had seen, of course, many camels in menageries, but they never impressed me as those free camels in their native wilds. Their appearance indicated that the great desert country was not far away; yet the road we were traversing was as smooth as ever, and the driver of mules did not relax his efforts to put us into Tlemcen on time. Along in the afternoon we climbed the outermost brim of the valley in which Tlemcen is situated, and saw it before us. a fair city of mosques and minarets, rising from leafy gardens. Of course our driver had reserved his greatest efforts for the final spurt, and we clattered into the city in a cloud of dust, and rolled up to the *bureau de poste* in a perfect halo of glory.

A YOUNG MOOR.

I was pounced upon by two Arab boys, immediately after I alighted, and led off to look at a fine room a lady friend of theirs had for rent. But this *belle chambre* I found dark and dingy, and though the woman seemed very much in need of money, I did not consider it my duty to incommode myself for her advantage. So I was led around to the Hôtel de la Paix, and there installed at ten francs per day. As my stay was to be limited, I bargained with a guide, that very night, to conduct me through Tlemcen on the morrow. His name was Mahomet, and he may have been as virtuous as his great namesake, but I doubt it. He wore baggy breeches, which were continually wobbling from side to side, a short Turkish jacket, a red fez, and Turkish slippers, with his calves and ankles bare. He was my guide through the city.

And what is Tlemcen, that I should take the trouble to seek it out? Tlemcen is unique. It is a Moorish or Arab city, of ancient date, and with architectural monuments that remind one of the Alhambra.

A MOORISH GENERAL.

As I came into Algiers in order to acquaint myself with the Moorish architecture and Moorish customs, merely as an introductory to the Arabic architecture of Spain, I sought out Tlemcen as containing the highest expression of the art. Tlemcen, in Roman days, was known as Pomaria, from its gardens of fruit-trees.

It was just about eleven hundred years ago that the Arab city was founded here, upon the ruins of what the Vandals had left. During four hundred years Tlemcen (which included a double town known as Aghadir and Tagrart) enjoyed great prosperity. It was one of the most important of the Moslem cities of the Occident. It was a great commercial centre, and contained at one time, it is estimated, five thousand Christians, — Genoese, Catalan, and Venetian merchants, who occupied a portion of the city by themselves, known as the Kissaria. The city will be found to be surrounded with several lines of fortifications, not only for the defence of the city itself but for its investment, for it has been many times besieged, and also taken. In 1553 it was taken by the accursed Turks, and from that period dates its decay. From a literary and commercial centre, radiant with enlightening influences, it sank into nothingness. The French captured the place in 1836, but surrendered it to Abd-el-Kader in 1839, whose capital it was until 1842, when the French repossessed themselves of it, and it has remained in their power ever since.

Let us see, now, if Tlemcen has within its ruined walls enough of interest to warrant this long journey. Mahomet came for me early in the morning, and we started out in the delicious coolness upon our tour of inspection.

First, of course, Mahomet, being a good Mahometan, conducted me to the mosque, — the great mosque Djamaa-el-Kebir, in the place d'Alger. It is not notable above even the mosque in the city of Algiers, though its court is paved with Algerian onyx, and the basin of its fountain is of the same. It has seventy-two square columns and a beautiful *mihrab*, or prayer-niche, ornamented with arabesques. The minaret is about one hundred feet high, and from its cupola I got a view of the city that rewarded me for all the pains of the journey. The mosque dates from 1136, though built upon a foundation from the year 790.

"Tlemcen," wrote an Arab author of the fifteenth century, "is a city enjoying a pleasant climate and a fertile soil. Built on the side of a mountain, it reminds one of a fair young bride reposing in beauty on her nuptial couch. The bright foliage which overshadows the white roofs is like a green coronal encircling her majestic brow. The surrounding heights and the plain stretching below the town are made verdant by running streams. Tlemcen is a city that fascinates the mind and seduces the heart."

It was once the queen of Morocco; now it is severed from its ancient territory and belongs to the Gauls.

France controls now the northern coast of Africa, and doubtless, if the genius of the people may prevail, will some day possess as wide a realm as the poet describes: —

> "Where the stupendous Mountains of the Moon
> Cast their broad shadows o'er the realms of noon,
> From rude Caffraria, where the giraffes browse
> With stately heads among the forest boughs,
> To Atlas, where Numidian lions glow
> With torrid fire beneath eternal snow;
> From Nubian hills, that hail the dawning day,
> To Guinea's coast, where evening fades away;
> Regions immense, unsearchable, unknown,
> Bask in the splendor of the solar zone, —
> A world of wonders, where creation seems
> No more the works of Nature, but her dreams."

Another mosque may be found within the walls, though it is now used as a schoolroom. This is the Mosque of Sidi Ahmed Bel Hassan el Ghomari, and its *mihrab* is decorated with arabesque most beautiful and fanciful. I do not think I have seen better examples of airy tracery even in the Alhambra. The schoolmaster was away, but the door of the mosque was open; so Mahomet and I marched in, and I pitched my camera and took a photograph of the *mihrab*. This mosque is about six hundred years old.

Speaking of mosques, there are two, with very beautiful minarets, just outside and below the western wall. For the city is enclosed on every side by a high wall, with great gateways leading out, one toward Oran, the other toward the desert. The finer of the two is that of Sidi el Halani, or the Sweetmeat-maker, with a minaret decorated with mosaics and a great court with arabesques, and with columns of Algerian onyx. It has finely carved cedar ceilings, and is comparatively modern, being only about five hundred years old. This mosque lies under the hill, and as you descend you can look down upon the minaret and the court, and view the whole ground-plan of the buildings. Upon the square top of this minaret, as upon that of every tower in the city, the huge bulk of a stork's nest may be seen, with the great birds keeping watchful guard.

"Before the Arabian conquest," wrote Mungo Park, "or about the middle of the seventh century, all the inhabitants of Africa, whether descended from Numidians, Phœnicians, Carthaginians, Vandals, or Goths, were comprehended under the general name of *Mauri*, or Moors." All these nations were converted to the religion of Mahomet during the Arabian empire under the caliphs. Among the first converts must have been the dwellers in and about this ancient city of Tlemcen, for we find tombs of the saints there over a thousand years old, if reports may be trusted.

I have called Tlemcen a "City of Arab Saints," because it was the dwelling-place of many venerated men whose tombs are now held as sacred places. About a mile distant from the city is the most venerated of them all, that of Sidi Bou Medine. Leaving the city by the gateway of Bou Medine, Mahomet and I passed many groups of females on their way to the cemetery. All were closely veiled, but we could not fail to notice that though their faces were covered their ankles were bare. They took no notice of us, but ambled along in that pokey way they have, and when they reached the cemetery they gathered in groups around various graves. The square tomb sacred to the memory of Sidi Snoosi, whom my guide called El Snoozer, seemed to be the favorite with them.

MUSICIANS OF MOROCCO.

I certainly thought they would display a little animation when I turned my camera upon them, but they only drew their coverings closer about them and squinted at me with half an eye. So I revenged myself by taking a photograph of them, even though several fierce-looking Arabs were prowling about and glaring at me as if yearning for my gore. I asked Mahomet what they gathered about the graves for, and he said it was the only chance in the week they had for gossip! I don't know what in the world they could find to gossip about, since every woman's costume is exactly like every other woman's, and they wear no bustles nor indulge in other luxuries and excrescences so dear to the average woman. But there they sat for an hour or more, almost immovable, and if they gossiped they did so in a quiet, lady-like way, squatted there on their haunches, without even a cup of tea to promote the flow of speech.

In their every act these Arabs are quiet and dignified. I choose to believe these women engaged in devotion. Of a similar scene some one has written: " Regarding the scene from a purely artistic point of view, we can imagine no more fitting subject for a painter than this group of Arabs at their devotions,— Nature their temple, its altar the setting sun, their faces toward Mecca, their hearts toward the Prophet, their every attitude breathing devotion and faith."

The cemetery is thickly set with graves, and one needs caution not to stumble over the numerous headstones, which are quaintly shaped and carven, and many of them picked out in colors, red, green, or yellow. A solemn place, this, and conducive to reflection, with its many memorials of the dead and its venerable olive-trees. It should be seen by moonlight, however, to be most effective; then indeed does it suggest an unreal city by the banks of the quiet river.

Beyond the graveyard is the Mosque of Sidi Bou Medine, entered by a narrow way, sometimes closed by doors of bronze,— doors of such exquisite workmanship as to suggest the highest art. The pattern is an interlaced geometric, and they remind me of the bronze doors of the Mosque of Cordova. The decoration of the mosque is good, but much is modern, and in effect is somewhat tawdry.

Stepping down below the level of the court, we enter the *Koubba* of the saint himself, Bou Medine, called the patron saint of Tlemcen. This tomb is approached through a small court, in which is a well with curbing of stone which has been deeply worn by the use of seven hundred years. An old Arab sat here, guarding this sacred place from unbelievers who should venture to approach with feet uncovered.

Sidi Bou is said to have been born in Spain, in Seville, when it was under Moslem rule, in the year of the Hegira 520, or A. D. 1126. He came over to Fez and studied theology, and died near Tlemcen. The interior of the tomb is hung with silken draperies, banners that are said to have been taken in Spain, ostrich-eggs, and other offerings of the sons of the Desert. In one corner is an object seemingly incongruous, and that is a grandfather's clock. How many years it has ticked away the time in that ancient tomb no one knows. Directly in front of the entrance-way to the outer court rises that of the mosque itself, ornamented with mosaic tiles made in Morocco.

Everywhere, even in this most sacred place of the Arabs, I was treated with respect, and received with a grave courtesy that would have repelled the idea of a fee — had it not been for the ever-extended palm.

Sidi Bou has a delightful situation, and the surrounding Arab village, though dirty, is yet charming in little stone houses and walled vineyards and gardens.

On our way back we made a détour that took in another holy *koubba*, in a delightful cemetery, that of Sidi-Yakoub, which is of

TLEMCEN.

the general shape and symmetry of the tombs of Blidah, in the sacred olive-grove. Not far from this is the great minaret of the Aghadir, a mosque long since destroyed, and which is over a thousand years old.

These lofty minarets, so graceful and so tall, set the Professor to making a comparison with towers and monuments in other parts of the world. The following are the heights of a few of the tallest of them: The Leaning Tower of Pisa, 179 feet; Baltimore, Washington Monument, 210; Montreal, Nôtre Dame Cathedral, 220; Boston, Bunker Hill Monument, 221; Montreal, English Cathedral, 224; Paris, Notre Dame, 224; Bologna, leaning tower, 272; Cairo, minaret of Mosque of Sultan Hassan, highest Mahometan minaret in the world, 282; New York, Trinity Church, 284; Florence, Campanile, or Giotto's Tower, 292; Lincoln, Cathedral, 300; Washington, Capitol, 307; Venice, Campanile, 322; New York, St. Patrick's Cathedral (to be when completed), 330; Utrecht, Cathedral (formerly 364), 338; Florence, Cathedral, 352; Milan, Cathedral, 355; London, St. Paul's, 365; Brussels, Hôtel de Ville, 370; Lubeck, Cathedral, 395; Antwerp, Cathedral, 402; Amiens, Cathedral, 422; Hamburg, St. Michael's, 428; Landshut, St. Martin's, 435; Cairo, Pyramid of Chefren, 446; Vienna, St. Stephen's, 449; Cairo, Pyramid of Cheops (original height, 480), 450; Rome, St. Peter's, 455; Rouen, Nôtre Dame, 465; Strasburg, Cathedral, 468; Hamburg, St. Nicholas', 473; Cologne, Cathedral, 511; Washington Monument, 555.

Were it not that I am about to describe another minaret yet more magnificent, I should halt to admire this impressive structure. All about the plains and slopes this side Tlemcen are the ruins of walls, towers, and minarets. These circles of fortifications can yet be made out surrounding the present city. That afternoon I again placed myself in charge of Mahomet, and we went out exploring in a different quarter. At first we lost ourselves in the network of ravines and fortifications that lies between the town and the hills behind it. Then we emerged upon an open field, gay with scarlet poppies and dotted with knotted old olive-trees. Climbing away beyond, our pathway led up the cliff, several hundred feet high, and after much difficulty we reached a plateau above. Here I found another *koubba* placed upon the verge of the cliff, and visible from afar. This, Mahomet told me, is the tomb of a most holy woman, who had been dead not less than a thousand years. This I believe, for the Arabs have no respect for a woman less than a thousand years old. A little garden and fig-orchard lay around it, and here lived the guardian of the tomb with his little family. They received me well, and I chatted with them awhile and then hastened on. The view from this *koubba* is magnificent, taking in the whole valley in which Tlemcen is built, the mountains of Morocco beyond, and a faint glimmer of the distant sea. Down the face of this cliff fall two sparkling streams, one toward Tlemcen, and the other toward Mansoura.

Mansoura is another city, — a city that has perished, all but its walls. During one of the long sieges of Tlemcen, nearly six hundred years ago, the chief in command turned his military camp into a city by building around it a wall forty feet high, enclosing about two hundred and fifty acres. At points about one hundred feet apart high towers were erected, battlemented and pierced. From the plateau I counted eighty towers yet remaining. It was a beautiful scene, — that broad plain bounded by hills, in its centre the twin cities Tlemcen and Mansoura, the one living, the other dead.

High above the walls and towers rises the great minaret to the mosque that Abou Yakoub commanded to be built. It is about one hundred and twenty feet high, and called "by far the most beautiful architectural monument of Moorish times in Algeria." It is half in ruins, but has been strengthened by the French. It resembles the great tower of Seville, the Giralda; and, like that

AT THE END OF A JOURNEY.

tower, its ascent is made by a series of ramps instead of stairs, so that a horseman might ride to the summit.

Were this the only monument here, tourists would come to view this grand memorial of the Moors. As to its color: "Photographs may help you a little to imagine the place; but having looked at them, you must shut your eyes and color minaret and walls with richest reddest ochre; you must clothe the hills in living green, fill the space between hill and heavens with soft warm skies of southern blue, and then set the whole picture floating and palpitating in golden mist. This minaret is unlike anything else in the world. It is like a gigantic monolith of solid Indian gold, and is as wonderful as the Pyramids."

We returned to the city through the Gate of Fez, leaving behind us this dead city, whose walls once enclosed great palaces and gardens, leaving it to the few Arabs now encamped within its fortifications. It was such a delight to wander around the angles of its towers, beneath the shade of half-wild olives, and through peaceful fields of wheat! The air was pure and bracing,—though the sun was hot,—and filled with flower-perfume and the hum of bees. It had been "one of those celestial days when heaven and earth meet and adorn each other; it seems a poverty that we could only spend it once."

We had as a guide an Arab named Amedi Omche, who was an appendage of the Hôtel de la Paix. If we had his autograph we would insert it; but as we have not, we give one of our little bills at the hotel itself.

GRAND HÔTEL DE LA PAIX

TENU PAR

PAUL BAILLS

TLEMCEN

Doit M *Nos* 9

TLEMCEN, le 2ᵐᵉ Mars, 1888.

DATES.	DÉSIGNATION.	SOMMES.
31	Dîner chambre . . .	6 00
1ᵉʳ Avril	1 journée, 1 café .	9 60
2	1 journée, 1 café	9 60
3	1 café au lait . . .	60
	Total	25 80

Returning to the city, we passed the remainder of the day in the streets and market-places, chaffing and chatting with the natives. The market was of the primitive kind, where vegetables were found in one corner, meat in another, and articles of domestic manufacture in another. All the marketing is done in the morning, and by noon the place is swept and garnished for health's sake; for these Arabs are now under French rule, and can no longer sit all day in the sun and fester and emit evil odors. But the most interesting of all is the Arab quarter, where the streets are narrow, where the shopkeepers sit all day in little dens about eight by ten feet square, each one with a different article for sale. Here we see the different handicraftsmen at work, — the shoemaker, who makes those wondrous slippers without heels, of gorgeous red and yellow, ornamented with gold and silver braid, and the tailor, whose duties are not very arduous, as all his costumes are of the same pattern.

It is thoroughly Oriental, and yet African. In these dens you find groups of gentlemanly Arabs, who are glad to have you join them in a cup of coffee and help them "at doing nothing all day in a row."

An English writer says of these same Arabs:—

"Years elapsed between our first and our last visit; yet there they were when we came again, *still doing nothing in a row.* There was the same old negro in a dark corner, making coffee and handing it to customers sitting in the same places, in the same dream.

"They have their traditions, their faith, their romance of life, and the curious belief that if they fear God and Mahomet, and *sit there long enough*, they will one day be sent for to Spain, to re-people the houses where their fathers dwelt.

"In such places as these we fall asleep and dream,—under the combined influences of coffee, hashish, the tom-tom, and heat,—dream that the world is standing still, and that all the people *in a hurry are dead!*"

CHAPTER VIII.

THE "DIAMOND IN AN EMERALD SETTING."

AT last we were in Algiers, city of the ancient Turkish corsairs. Our guide was an Arab, but evidently an honest one, not of the street variety, but of the desert. As a type of nearly all the Arab porters that swarm the streets and quays of Algiers he may now be presented. His complexion was a rich brown (or the coat of dirt that covered it was); above his complexion he wore a fez that was originally red, but now auburn; his person was clad in gunny-bags. One gunny-bag with three holes in it served as a shirt, another gunny-bag with two holes in the bottom served as pantaloons and was lashed around the waist with a scarf. Yet he seemed happy, almost as happy as other porters who wore more gunny-bags, and were consequently higher up in the social scale.

He trotted off ahead of us with our heap of luggage as though it was of no consequence at all. Owing to some defect in his understanding, he couldn't comprehend my French, neither could I understand his Arabic; but he knew well that I wanted to go to a hotel, and so he led the way to an imposing structure on the Boulevard, known as the Grand Hôtel d'Oasis. Oasis, as I learned once from my geography, means a "green spot in a desert," and as the name seemed refreshing, I allowed him to convey me thither. It was after the French style; all the hotels are of this kind throughout Algiers. The café is independent, or semi-detached; the office is near the entrance; an open hall, or *patio*, extends from the first floor nearly or quite to the roof, and the landlord awaits you with profound bows and a smiling countenance. In a very short time I was installed, my gunny-bag Arab was paid (another franc), and I was at liberty to saunter about the city.

First, as it was then early, I secured a cup of coffee and an orange, then strolled about to acquaint myself with the salient features of Algiers. It was a bright, cool, and windy morning, that of the 20th of March. Though early, a large proportion of the population seemed to be astir, and we had company everywhere; yet not an obtrusive company. The population of Algiers, Arab, Moor, Nubian, French, etc., is thoroughly cosmopolitan; it manifests no surprise at anything, for there never was, certainly, anything more unique than itself.

But the city. We must have a framework for our pictures, even though it be somewhat of a skeleton. In a word, as to situation, as to composition, as to surroundings, Algiers is the most beautiful of any we had then seen. Its beauty is of the Oriental type, with an intrusion from France. The French structures, which are mainly along the quays and in the lower part of the town, are of themselves fine, even grand, but they spoil the picture of Algiers from the sea by breaking the continuity of the converging lines that lead up the hillside from the water's edge.

In general outline this city is an isosceles triangle, resting against a background of red and verdure-clad hills. Not inaptly, the ancient Arabs compared it to a *diamond with emerald setting*. A milky opal, rather, it seemed to me, with the hues of iridescence clouded over; for the walls and roofs are creamy-hued, and from a little distance blend most beautifully with their surroundings. The general slope of the Sahel, or chain of hills, behind and extending beyond the city is toward the south and east. From the blue waters of the deep bay the city mounts the hill in a succession of terraces line above line, the modern French houses near the water-line, the true Arab city higher up, and the apex of the pyramid crowned by the Kasba, or ancient citadel of the Beys, some four hundred feet above the quays. Since the French occupation of Algiers, now some

AN OASIS IN THE DESERT.

fifty years past, the modern buildings above the entire water-front have been erected. The most magnificent work here seems to be along the quays, a series of arches rising some forty feet above the water-line, in two tiers, covering an area of eleven acres, with a frontage of thirty-seven hundred feet, and occupied as warehouses and storage-rooms, some three hundred and fifty in number. This great work was the achievement of Sir Morton Peto; it cost some £300,000, and was completed about twenty years ago. This system of arches supports the grand avenue formerly called the Boulevard de l'Impératrice (Eugénie), but now known as the Boulevard de la République. As it overlooks the enclosed harbor, the beautiful bay, the shipping, and gives glimpses of the Atlas Mountains beyond, this boulevard is the favorite promenade of an afternoon and evening, and is densely crowded. The finest buildings, six to eight stories in height, front toward this boulevard and the bay, and the best hotels are here, nearly all with a line of arcades.

All the buildings of the city are of stone, massive structures, many with white or tinted walls, and roofs of tiles. There is no structure in the world that lends itself so perfectly to become a component part of the landscape as the stone-walled building with roof of richly tinted tiles. I wonder why we do not use this kind more in America. Is it because of the frost, or expense, or custom to the contrary? To counterbalance our evil of frost, they have here the gales of the Mediterranean and an occasional earthquake.

An unbroken line of fortifications surrounds the city, beginning at either end of the boulevard, running up the hills behind it and crowning its crest, — a high wall, loopholed, battlemounted, and buttressed by occasional forts. Two great jetties sweep around from north and south and enclose a sheltered harbor two hundred and twenty-two acres in area, with a depth of forty feet, and a width of entrance something over one thousand feet. The breakwater was begun in 1836, and is said to have been the first experiment in constructing works of this kind with blocks of concrete. It was a successful experiment, and even though some of the great blocks have been undermined and broken down, the enclosed harbor is perfectly sheltered. Beacons at either extremity, one showing a green and the other a red light, guide the mariner into the harbor at night. All this was a modern work; but there had existed, previous to the coming of the French, a small harbor protected by a mole. This was constructed in 1518, by the first of the pirate Deys who made the name of Algiers such a terror to the followers of the sea.

Not only the remains of this are still seen, but even the lighthouse built in 1544 yet stands. It is octagonal in shape, one hundred and twenty feet high, and displays a fixed white light visible fifteen miles at sea. This lighthouse of the pirates is built upon the remains of a fort the Spaniards erected and held for many years, called by them Fort Peñon. The fortifications, as already mentioned, begin at the breakwater on either side and entirely enclose, not alone the city, but the hill on which it is built. A great wall was built from the sea to the Kasba in 1540 by one of the pachas, and in 1581 the fort at the eastern end of the Boulevard de la République, known as the Fort Bab-Azoun. The present line of environment consists of a high rampart, parapet, and ditch, with here and there bastions stretching around from sea to sea. To the north is the city gate of Bab-el Oned, to the south the gate of Bab-Azoun. These modern fortifications are said to have cost above two million dollars, and occupy about one hundred and eighty acres; yet they are of little use at the present time, and are more effective as picturesque features of the town's architecture than as means of defence.

Having now got the city surrounded, let us note something of its history. The highest point on the fortified line is the great Fort de l'Empéreur, built some three hundred and fifty years ago by Hassan Pacha, the successor to Kheir-ed-din. They were the first of the long line of Deys. Very few of these rulers had a very long reign, as they were either strangled, or stabbed, or thrown into the sea. Their stronghold was the citadel crowning the triangular city, the Kasba, from the high pavilion of which they overlooked the city, the bay, and the open sea beyond. This Kasba was an immense structure, part of which is still standing, with a mosque and interior palace, defended, it is said, by above two hundred pieces of artillery.

Such was the stronghold of the Algerine corsairs; let us see what history says of them. From the opening chapter in Sir R. L. Playfair's "Scourge of Christendom" I extract the following:

"Even as early as 1390, the Barbary corsairs began to trouble the seas, and at the urgent request of the Genoese a force consisting of a 'great number of lords, knights, and gentlemen of France and England set out from Genoa' to chastise them. . . . They landed at Mehedia, on the coast of Tunis, where the English archers did good service with their long bows, beating back the enemy from the shore. They besieged Mehedia, but at length, constrained with the intemperancy of the scalding air in that hot country, breeding in the army sundry diseases, they fell to a compensation on certain articles, and so sixty-one days after their arrival they returned home."

After the fall of Granada, in 1492, the ravages of the pirates became more serious. A considerable number of Moorish families settled in North Africa; they were too much exasperated against their persecutors not to seek every opportunity for revenge, and being well acquainted with the coasts of their native country, their fury naturally fell upon the Spaniards nearest the Mediterranean. But it was not confined to these alone. English traders were great sufferers; indeed, the Moors openly avowed themselves the common enemies of Christendom.

Ferdinand of Spain became seriously alarmed; in 1509 his fleets took possession of Oran and Bonzia, and a force was sent to reconnoitre Algiers; but finding nothing there save a small harbor and a walled *enciente*, they merely occupied one of the islands, subsequently called El Peñon, which they strongly fortified.

Algiers derives its name, it is said, from these islands in its harbor (*El Djezair*, — the islands). The Spaniards were thus enabled to blockade the port, to prevent the entrance or departure of a piratical craft, and force the Algerines to pay tribute. At the death of Ferdinand, in 1516, the Algerines made an attempt to recover their liberty. They offered the sovereignty of their city to Salem, at Numi, an Arab from Blidah, who at once began to blockade the Peñon and prevent all provisions from being supplied to it from the town. The fort retaliated by cannonading the town; and in this emergency Salem sent an embassy to invite the celebrated corsairs, Baba Arondji, or Barbarossa, and his brother (Greeks of Mitylene, who had settled at Djidjely) to come to Algiers and assist in expelling the Spaniards.

Baba Arondji was only too happy to embrace this opportunity of making himself master of Algiers. He advanced upon it by land with five thousand men; soon after, he strangled the Emir with his own hands, forced his wife to commit suicide, and massacred all the women of his harem. He took possession of the place nominally as a vassal of the Sultan, but really as an independent ruler. In 1518 Barbarossa was killed in an encounter with the Spaniards at Rio Salado, near Tlemcen, and was succeeded at Algiers by his brother, Kheir-ed-din. In 1529 the latter succeeded in taking the Peñon fort from the Spaniards, killing or enslaving its garrison, and putting to death its brave commander, Martin de Vargas. He at once deprived it of its insular position by joining it to the mainland by means of a causeway, thus forming the harbor, or mole, destined for so many years to give shelter to the pirate fleets.

The history of Algiers as a piratical State really begins with the reign of Kheir-ed-din, in 1518. For three hundred years it was governed by the Turks, and held all the nations of Europe in terror. Year by year the depredations of the Barbary corsairs became more audacious. They could not support themselves without roaming the sea for plunder, which they did, without the least fear or apprehension, as far even as the shores of England. At other times, carrying with them renegades as guides, they deliberately landed on the coasts and islands of the Mediterranean, pillaged towns and farms, and carried off their inhabitants into most wretched captivity. In this manner they utterly ruined Corsica, Sardinia, Sicily, many parts of the coast of Italy and Spain, and the Balearic Islands. They arrogated to themselves the right to wage war on every nation of Europe which did not purchase their forbearance by tribute or special treaties, and they absolutely declined to be on friendly terms with more than one or two at a time, so that they might be free to plunder the remainder. They dictated the most humiliating conditions and restrictions in matters concerning the internal affairs of the Christian powers, especially with regard to their navigation laws, such as the nature of the passes their vessels were to carry, and the number of foreigners allowed to be on board; and they successfully maintained their right to search all vessels on the high seas. They never hesitated to send the representatives of the most powerful monarchs to hard labor in chains at the quarries, or even to blow them away from guns at the smallest provocation.

It seems incredible at the present day that such a state of things could have been permitted to exist. The only explanation is that our nation found these corsairs a convenient scourge for others with whom it was at war. Thus the consuls of the various nations, but especially those of England and France, were perpetually scheming to induce the Dey to break peace with the rival nation or to prevent its restoration after war had actually broken out.

The whole history of the Algerines shows that they never respected any treaty when they could violate it with advantage or probable immunity; nevertheless, they continued to be treated till the very last, by all the maritime nations, with a degree of respect to which they never had any just claim. Even England, France, and Spain paid tribute, if not directly, then through the form of consular presents, and most valuable gifts in money and warlike stores. The weaker nations, which had to submit to the humiliation of paying actual tribute, were treated in the most contemptuous manner, and in the event of too long arrears remaining unpaid, their consuls were sent to hard labor in chains, from which some of them actually died. Mr. Eaton, American consul at Tunis, said in 1798, writing of the Dey: "Can any man believe that this elevated brute has seven kings of Europe, two republics, and a continent tributary to him, when his whole naval force is not equal to two line-of-battle ships?" On the other hand, every State in Europe held it lawful at one time to enslave an infidel; the common law of England, as well as the Inquisition, doomed heretics to the stake. The Inquisition was what, doubtless, drove first the Moors to make these reprisals for the terrible sufferings of their ancestors.

Until 1618 Algiers was governed by a Pasha, in direct subordination to the Porte. At this date the Sultan consented to his being nominated by the militia, but reserved the right of confirmation. In 1661 the Janissaries gave the actual authority to their own Agha, and in 1671 they elected one of their own body as Dey, or Protector. From that time the Pasha sent by the Porte had to content himself with the honors of his position, without exercising any real power. From 1710 the title of Pasha was conferred on the Dey, and the two offices became united in the same person.

In regard to slavery, one author says:—

"When that institution was at its height, there were from twenty thousand to thirty thousand captives at a time in Algiers alone, representing every nation in Europe and every rank in society, from the viceroy to the common sailor,— men of the highest eminence in the church, literature, science, and arms, delicately nurtured ladies and little children, doomed to spend their lives in infamy. The majority never returned to their native land, and comparatively few have

DECATUR'S FIGHT WITH THE ALGERIAN.

left us a detailed account of their sufferings. The slaves were either the property of the Dey or of private individuals. They were sold at auction. The government slaves generally wore a ring of iron around one ankle, and were bound in three prisons, or bagnios, in dark cells, swarming with vermin. In every bagnio there was a small chapel, and the slaves were allowed the free exercise of their religion. Words cannot paint their miserable condition; yet, deplorable as it was, there is no reason to suppose that it was worse than that of the galley slaves of France, Spain, Italy, or Malta. We may search in vain for records of greater cruelty than the tortures inflicted during the reign of Louis XIV. on the Huguenot prisoners during their long and painful marches from Paris to the coast, where as many as four hundred were sometimes fastened together by the neck, couple behind couple, to a long central chain, till they were finally consigned to the unspeakable tortures of the royal galleys at Toulon or Marseilles."

After the subjection of Algiers to the Christian powers in the early part of this century, the Turks, the masters of the country until then, did not exceed three thousand men, wrote our consul-general, Mr. Shaler, in 1816; that is, the number in the Regency eligible for any office of honor or profit.

The number of *Kouloughis* (or descendants of Turks and Moorish women) was about twelve thousand. This latter class had some privileges, but not a common feeling with the Turks. Besides these, there was a small body of seamen, generally native Algerines. The rest of the population consisted of Moors, Arabs, Biscaries, Kabyles, and Jews, enjoying no rights, and subject to every sort of oppression.

At that time, in 1816, Algiers received one hundred and thirty thousand dollars a year from tributary powers, including fifty thousand dollars from Great Britain. The Algerine commerce was too insignificant to be mentioned, any deficiency being more than made good by plunder. "Of their too celebrated navy, a brig, a schooner, and seven gunboats only remained after the bombardment."

It was about a hundred years ago, or in 1783, that Algiers

declared war against the United States, in order to make prizes of its merchant vessels. Ten years later more than one hundred Americans were in slavery, and our minister to Portugal was empowered to negotiate a treaty for their liberation. By this treaty we paid the pirates seven hundred thousand dollars, and were further pledged to pay an annual tribute of twenty thousand dollars. In the last year of the last century the Algerines made an insulting demand of Captain Bainbridge, commanding the frigate "George Washington," but it was not until 1812 that they again declared open war against us.

Other nations had endured their insults for centuries, but the United States, as soon as possible, or in 1815, resolved to break the chains and bring the Dey of Algiers to terms. Bainbridge and Decatur were sent there with a squadron, and forced the pirate to a recognition of American rights, at the same time landing William Shaler as consul-general. The full account of these proceedings may still be seen at the American consulate in Algiers.

The next year the English, encouraged by American success, sent a squadron under Lord Exmouth, who bombarded the city, firing into it over fifty thousand shot and shell, and inflicting a loss upon the Algerines of over seven thousand. By this means he succeeded in liberating three thousand slaves, of all nations;

STEPHEN DECATUR.

but it was not long before the pirate corsairs were again sweeping the seas for plunder from the Christians.

It is a wonder that the civilized world had so long permitted this Turkish ulcer to exist, when one vigorous application of the knife would have removed it. But it was left for the French to put an end forever to Turkish rule in Algiers.

It was upon a trivial pretext that they declared war against Algiers; but it served the purpose, and in June, 1830, thirty-four thousand men were landed. On the 4th of July they captured the forts commanding the city, and on the 10th the Dey embarked with all his suite and harem for Naples.

CHAPTER IX.

IN THE CORSAIRS' STRONGHOLD.—THE DOCTOR TELLS AN INDIAN STORY.

 HAVE more still to say about Algiers and the Algerines; but at this juncture the Doctor claims my attention, and says that I am putting in too many statistics, and he thinks he should have a word to say. Perhaps he may be right; at all events, I will let him tell his story, and our readers may sit in judgment on him. The Doctor, as you know, is a rather light-headed individual, but he means well, and he has travelled extensively. The story he tells here is of the time when he was a reporter on a Boston paper, and the editor sent him off to write about the Indians.

"Boston is at present the most monotonous place in the universe," said the managing editor to me, as I appeared before him, in response to his invitation; "there has actually nothing exciting occurred since that man was stabbed on the Common."

"Had his nose slit, did n't he?"

"Yes, about six months ago. Well, what I want now is something stirring, something to break this universal sameness; and you are the man I have selected to break it. Not a word; it must be broken. When can you start?"

"Hot or cold country?"

"What 's the difference?"

"All equipped for a hot climate,—light clothing, cholera mixture, and bitters; but a cold country settles me, for my overcoat's in pawn."

"That decides it, then; it's a hot country, — Mexico."

"What portion?"

"The northern first, Chihuahua; but eventually the whole."

"Beg pardon; Chee — what?"

"Chihuahua; you must exercise on these Mexican words. With this one you attempt first to sneeze, then begin a war-whoop, but bite it off in the middle."

"Thank you; but I might bite off more than I could chaw."

"Could what?"

"Chew."

"Ah! um? Let me see. Here are your railroad passes to the Mexican border, a letter to the general manager of the Central Railroad, a thirty-eight calibre six-shooter, bottle of pain-killer, and a corkscrew. Won't that do you for a send-off?"

"You 've forgotten one thing."

"Oh, certainly, my blessing, which I freely give you."

"Can I realize on it?"

"Realize?"

"Convert it into cash!"

"True, I forgot that; here's a draft for —— dollars. One word more; in writing of Mexico, always allude to it as 'Our Sister Republic;' our aim is to create a fraternal feeling between the Gringo and the Greaser, and it's better to pat the Mexican on the back than to pull his hair. Again, never fail to observe that every important enterprise in the West owes its inception to Boston capital; never forget that the simple word Boston is an open sesame to the hospitality of the haughty don and — and the humble donkey. Go now: remember that Boston follows you; that our eye is on you. Your first adventure will be with the Apaches."

"But, my dear sir, the Apaches are Indians."

"To be sure, we have thousands of them on the reservations; but the genuine, Simon-pure Apache is only to be found in Mexico. What we want is, the wild man in a state of nature, as he exists without civilization and fire-water; give us real adventure, something hair-lifting! And don't peddle out to us that stock story of the United States never having kept faith with a single redskin in any of its treaties; we want an Indian that has never been treatied. And no gush about the 'Great Father at Washington;' I can put that in myself; all that sort of thing we keep in stock, to trot out occasionally, for the benefit of the Peace Societies."

"It's very kind of you, I'm sure; but the sort of Indian you are yearning for generally resents all intrusion into his domain."

"That's your business; fortunately you're pretty bald — you've been married twice, I believe, — and no sensible Indian will attach much importance to your scalp."

With these words the managing editor bowed me out; two days later I was in Chicago, the third night in Kansas City, and within a week had placed twenty-eight hundred miles between me and Boston. Diligent inquiry, after I had arrived in the capital of Chihuahua — a large and quaint old Mexican city — revealed the fact that a strong armed force was about to start in pursuit of the Apaches, whose stronghold was in the fastnesses of the Sierra Madre Mountains, some two hundred miles distant.

The officer in command of this force, the Thirteenth Regiment of the Mexican Army of the North, was extremely kind and courteous, and by a judicious use of my Spanish (which I had acquired a mastery of in South America), supplemented by the corkscrew, I obtained his permission to accompany them.

Our band of soldiers was composed entirely of Indians, mainly Aztecs from the Valley of Mexico, nearly as dark in complexion as mulattoes, undersized, clad in ragged and dirty regimentals, but carrying excellent rifles, which they could use effectively; and they were the best fighters in the world. They marched with a rapid pace, keeping up easily with our wiry mustangs, never seemed tired, and were always cheerful. Their total pay was about a *real* (twelve cents) a day. By a liberal use of cigarettes and tobacco, with a little *mescal*, or Mexican rum, now and then, I gained the good will of these poor devils so completely, that a detachment of them was ready at any time to go off with me wherever I might wish to lead them.

We were going to penetrate into the Mexican State of Sonora, where, hidden among the almost inaccessible mountains, were a few fertile valleys, occupied from time immemorial by the Apaches, — their secure retreat after all their murderous frays. These Indians rarely cultivate the soil, but rely mainly upon its natural products, such as the fruit of the cactus, the *piñon*, or pine nut, and especially a kind of oak which grows there, and bears a sweet acorn, which they grind into flour and make into bread. Sometimes they raise a few beans, corn, and pumpkins, vary their diet with stolen horse-flesh, and with canned goods taken from the white man, and drink immoderately the various liquors distilled from the Maguey plant. They are very fleet of foot, excellent horsemen, unerring shots both with bow and rifle, and many of the warriors still carry shields of leopard-skin, each with a mirror in its centre, to dazzle the eyes of an enemy.

Their warfare consists in surprises and attacks, they use signal-smokes, and still make fire by that primitive method of twirling a hard, pointed stick in a softer one. Their best and most courageous man is always their chief, head-ing the councils and leading them to battle. They go nearly naked, and are filthy to the last degree. The women never wash themselves or comb their hair while the "bucks" are on the war-path, — and they are on the war-path nearly all the time. They have only dim notions of a Supreme Being, whom they call Tax-tax-i-tax-i-tamme, but whom they never worship.

As fighters, they surpass any Indians in the United States; they have been known to ambuscade on a perfectly level plain, where there was neither brush nor tree, cover themselves with dust, tie grass to their hair to make it look like the clumps of grass about them, and in this way lie in wait for a wagon train, let it pass close to them, and then jump up and massacre the teamsters. When on the war-trail, they march seventy or eighty miles a day, by killing their horses as fast as they give out and stealing others from the ranches on the way. In this way they carry terror to wide sections of country, never halting, appearing in places far apart as if by magic, and retreating with their booty, when pursued, to the unknown fastnesses of the mountains we were seeking to penetrate.

Two years before, that great Indian fighter, General Crook, made a most perilous march down into a portion of this region from the north, and was absent so long, without sending out any tidings of his progress, that he was given up for lost, with all his band. But he finally came out, having captured two or three hundred Apaches, whom he placed on the reservation, where they were later followed by nearly all the *Barbaros* (Mexican savages) in the Sierras. All those at present residing in the United States are peaceful, and fast becoming civilized, having been supplied with agricultural implements, cows, and garden seeds, by the Indian agents, and having already raised very creditable crops of wheat and corn. At first, to be sure, they sacrificed all their cows and calves to their inordinate appetites, thinking it was a waste of meat to have it running about where some other Indians might capture it.

They have improved their leisure moments since General Crook brought them out of the wilderness of sin and iniquity into the light of civilization, and have become adepts at the national games of the Americans, such as euchre and poker. The fascinating Mexican game of *monté* they had already acquired before Crook found them, and passed whole days and nights in play. It was my good fortune to meet this band of savages as it was first brought over the Border. When in their native stronghold they were in the condition of poor Robinson Crusoe on his desolate island, — with more money than they knew what to do with (obtained from their forays upon the settlements), and with no market for the ponies and cattle they had stolen from the despised Mexicans. Thanks, however, to the solicitude of General Crook, they had at last been placed in communication with a market for their gains. Doubtless they commended themselves for their foresight in gathering to themselves much plunder against the time when they should be led out to trade in the white man's country. At all events, they had several thousand dollars of murdered men's money; and some Western gamblers, hearing of this, started for their camps with the laudable purpose of relieving them of the care of so much lucre. I wished them all success, and watched them engage the Indians in a game of *monté* with a good deal of interest. At first it was difficult to see which displayed the most skill, red-skin or pale-face; but the fount from which the former drew seemed inexhaustible, for Uncle Sam is president of the Indian bank, and when the present supply should be exhausted they had only to draw a check for more; in other words, take their government rifles and ammunition, sally out and bag a few worthless white settlers, and return to the fold with their spoil. But their long days of idleness on the reservation had not counted for nothing, as those gamblers learned; for when the shades of evening fell, the latter wended their way homeward in a condition expressed by that much-abused Western word, *busted*.

General Crook thought he had bagged the entire Apache band; but there was one wily old chief who resisted all importunities and remained hidden, with his squaws and a few of the bravest of his tribe, in the northern ravines of the mountains, where the Americans had not been able to penetrate. He had remained quiet for some time after Crook's raid, but of late had begun to run in cattle and had murdered a few *rancheros*. It was this old cut-throat chief (Old *Juh*, I think they called him, — pronounced *Who*), whom we were after, with our half regiment of Mexican soldiers.

Our force was large, but we had difficult work before us; for old Juh was said to be intrenched in a vast cañon from which numerous lateral ravines led out, and it was the purpose of our officer in command to surround entirely the whole region, occupy not only the table-land above the cañon, but post soldiers in every ravine, closing all avenues of escape.

It was at the close of our sixth day's march; we had left behind us the hot and arid plains and the cooler foot-hills, and approached the mountain stronghold of the Indian braves. During the following day our columns were deployed and posted at their assigned positions; the next day, at dawn, the various lines commenced their advance toward the central point. It was about noon before our detachment, which was scrambling along the rugged walls of the cañon, discovered Indian signs nigh. How the sun beat down between those perpendicular walls! The intense heat caused us to throw aside everything not absolutely necessary. Suddenly, as we were picking our way over the blister-

AN EQUESTRIAN DANCE.

ing rocks, a sharp report rang out, which the cañon walls reverberated until it seemed like thunder. It had not yet died away before one of our soldiers dropped, all in a heap, across a bowlder, shot through the head. Perfect silence succeeded; not a foe was in sight. Only a thin wreath of smoke, curling above a cave-hollowed cliff, told whence the fatal shot had come. "To the rocks!" shouted our captain; "get a shelter, and every man for himself!" But even before we could do this another shot rang out, and another soldier plunged headlong down the steep. Fortunately, we were at a point a little higher than the savages, and by working our way carefully along, obtained detached points whence we could occasionally see a black head pop out, and thus were warned in time to avoid the bullets. They were evidently few in number, but all were sharp shooters, and three more of our little group were killed before we could get a single shot at them. Then we got in a straggling volley that killed at least two of them; but they were well intrenched, and for ten hours we waited in suspense for the arrival of our friends from the lower end of the cañon. A commotion in that direction then showed us that they were coming. The Indians observed it, and were so excited by it that two more exposed themselves and were shot down. Gradually our gallant Mexicans advanced up the gorge; the Indian situation was so desperate that the savages made a break, trying to scale the cliff above them.

"Bayonets!" yelled our captain, and sprang forward with revolver in hand, followed by every man, including myself. Every one there, except myself, had some deed of blood to avenge, either for himself or some murdered comrade, and could not be stopped by the fire of the desperate savages. There were seven of them; five of our poor fellows were stopped by their bullets, but our friends below now nearly met us at the objective point, and it was a matter of savage rivalry as to who should first plunge his bayonet into the red-skin. I don't believe one "buck" escaped. Old Juh was the last; he backed himself into a cleft in the cliff and kept us back awhile, till the magazine of his rifle was exhausted; but a bayonet pierced his brawny breast at last, and with a shriek of rage he dashed upon the Mexican who thrust it at him, and fell, impaled upon the rocks.

Silence ensued; our captain, wounded in the arm, with the smoke still curling from his revolver, sank breathless upon the dead body of an Indian. Just then a swarthy being glided stealthily out from beneath a rock, passed the officer, and plunged a glittering knife-blade deep into the throat of the soldier who had given the *coup de grace* to Juh. For a moment paralyzed, three of his comrades dashed forward, and another savage lay dead with the rest. It was a squaw, hideous in paint and wrinkles, but heroic in her nature, who had done a deed for which a civilized woman would have been lauded to the skies. This movement directed our attention to the place of her retreat, and there we found a group of squaws and children huddled together beneath an overhanging rock, like a bevy of captured quail. So murderously troublesome had these Apaches been, that the blood of our men was at the boiling point, and they sprang forward to put an end to these scowling savages; but our captain was a hero. "Stop!" he shouted; "they cannot harm us. Take them with us, and let them live. True, their deeds have been extremely bad, but we can afford to be merciful and cannot afford to be cruel, — much less to stain our hands knowingly with the blood of squaws and children."

The soldiers sullenly obeyed him. One by one they were drawn from their hiding-place, thirteen of them, glaring at us defiance, but speechless.

Still the sun beat down upon us; we were parched with thirst. The bugle sounded a retreat. Our dead were buried in crevices of the rocks, our wounded tenderly assisted; and bringing the plunder of the Indian camp with our captives, we painfully retraced our steps out of the cañon, camping that night in an open pine forest. Our stragglers and scouts came in before daylight; and from their reports, and the reluctant replies to our questionings of the squaws, we were led to believe that we had effectually disposed of the last of the barbarous Indians of the Sierras.

Now that the Doctor has had his say, let me continue with my description of Algiers.

I hope my readers will pardon me this long introduction to my *olla podrida*. The *olla*, you know, is composed of beef, mutton, chicken, bacon, lard, pig's feet, garlic, onions, and all kinds of vegetables; and the Spaniards say : —

No hay olla sin tocino,
Ni sermon sin San Agostino.

"No olla without its bacon, and no sermon without Saint Augustine."

Although Algiers had little commerce with distant ports, and little trade with the interior, yet the French found nearly ten million dollars in the treasury. They immediately set about the pacification of the country, working from the coast to the mountains and the interior; but it was nearly seventeen years before the insurrections

of Arabs and Kabyles were entirely suppressed. The greatest chief to oppose them was Abd-el-Kader, a direct descendant of the family of the Prophet, and a holy man who had performed a pilgrimage to Mecca. This wonderful man kept the fires of insurrection alight until his capture, in 1847. He was taken to France a prisoner, was released in 1852, after swearing upon the Koran that he would fight the French no more, and died in Damascus.

The country enjoyed twenty years of comparative peace and prosperity, but in 1871, at the time of the Franco-German war, the hill tribes broke out into rebellion, which was only quenched after long and terrible struggles with the returning troops from France. Some trouble has since been experienced in the desert country, where an exploring expedition was exterminated; but at present the traveller can pass with perfect safety throughout that portion of North Africa in possession of the French. The greatest drawbacks to progress have been natural causes, or rather the unnatural workings of Nature's forces, — such as earthquakes (of local occurrence), locusts, droughts, and resultant famines and pestilence. In 1866 and 1867 occurred a great flight of locusts, coming up from the desert, and then excessive drought, with occasional earthquakes. It is estimated that two hundred thousand persons perished.

The French are actively building *barrages* for the storing of water to obviate the effects of drought, and they do all they can to destroy the locusts; but against the earthquakes they are powerless. The great locust-cloud of a few years ago will be long remembered for its disastrous effect upon Algerian agriculture.

The grand promenade is along the Boulevard de la République, above the quays, beneath the corridors of the great hotels, and around the Place du Gouvernment. These wide French streets and boulevards are the cleanest and most pleasant thoroughfares; but the narrow lanes that branch out from them and climb the hill are by far the dirtiest and most interesting. Such are the Rue de la Kasba, the

Rue Kleber, Ben Ali, and La Mer Rouge. In the Rue de la Mer Rouge one must ascend by steps, five hundred in number, and of course no carriage can enter. But its steepness and steps offer no obstacle to the donkeys, who crowd you against the walls at unexpected corners and act as though they owned the entire alley. Cautiously threading your way along and up this tortuous street, you have glimpses of the Orient that will repay all your exertion; of Arab dens, swarms of half-naked children, rows of Arab shoes with their heels chopped off, peeps into dimly lighted dens, from the obscurity of which gleam out wolfishly the eyes of masculine Arabs, while a more tender light may at rare intervals gladden you from the orbs of some Moorish damsel.

If we climb high enough, we shall reach certain corners where we can look back over the roofs, and out through the rifts in the walls, to the shining sea beyond. Climbing yet higher, we reach the Kasba, the ancient palace of the Deys, the foundations of which were begun in 1506. It caps the summit of the hill, the apex of the shining triangle of white houses and mosques lying against the Sahel. It was formerly defended by two hundred pieces of artillery, and contained vast treasure, even at the capture by the French. A fine mosque and minaret stand near, and the ornamental tiles are yet to be seen, in places, suggestive of former elegance. Here dwelt those semi-savage Turks and Moors whose barbarities held Christians in awe for several centuries.

In the centre of the Place du Gouvernement is a fine equestrian statue of the Duke d'Orleans, and on one side a large mosque with a square minaret about ninety feet high, in which is a clock. This mosque, Djamaa el Djelid, was planned, it is said, by a Genoese, a prisoner here in 1660, who was promised liberty for his work; but as he made the ground-plan in the form of a cross, he only obtained his liberty by being literally blown from the mouth of a cannon. In the parlance of the day, he was fired. A more

DOOR OF MOSQUE OF BOU MEDINA.

ancient mosque, said to have been erected in the eleventh century, is the Djamaa el Kebir, in the Rue de la Marine, very near to the other. Its interior is like that of all mosques, with massive columns supporting the roof upon Moorish arches. Coarse matting covers the floors, and protects it from the foot of the unbeliever. At the entrance to every mosque, or in the court, is a fountain where the Moslems wash their feet before entering this holy place.

The Koran commands frequent ablution, though you would not believe it, looking at and smelling of the Arabs; and you may be pardoned for assuming that the nomadic Bedouin always takes advantage of the clause in the Koran that allows him to substitute *sand* for water. Washing with sand is not nearly as expensive or troublesome as washing with water,— especially in the Sahara.

A few lamps are hung here, and the only other objects to attract attention are the *mimbar*, or pulpit, and the *mihrab*, or holy niche toward Mecca. Of the mosque and the great square I one day secured a most interesting instantaneous photograph, just as a big black dog was crossing it, and a fine group of Moors were sweeping by in flowing robes.

More than a hundred mosques are said to have stood in Algiers previous to the French invasion, but doubtless many of them are merely *koubbas*. These may be seen dotting every hill-crest in the country, and occupying nearly every prominent situation in Algiers. The finest of these is that of Sidi Abd-er-Rahman, above the garden Marengo. This saint died in 1471, and his beautiful mausoleum is hung with the richest silk drapery, banners, lamps, and ostrich eggs. It is called the most ancient sacred edifice, excepting the great mosque, of North Africa. The cemetery in front and around it is charming, in its quaintest tombs and headstones, where rest the ashes of many Mahometan rulers, the latest interred there being the Dey of Constantine. Below this enclosed cemetery lies an attractive spot,— the Jardin Marengo,— where many strange plants flourish, where serpentine walks lead to glorious outlooks over the sea, and where coolness and shade ever invite the traveller to rest. In its centre stands an ornamental kiosk, decorated, and with fanciful tiles. Speaking of religious edifices, we should not neglect the French Cathedral, in the Place Malakoff, built on the site of the Mosque of Hassan. A broad flight of twenty-three steps leads to the entrance, within the portico, with its four black-veined marble columns. It is eligibly situated, though the small square in front is frequently filled with Arabs from the country, and men and women coming to market.

More conspicuous, both from its position and its architecture, is the famous Church of Our Lady of Africa, perched upon a commanding promontory a short distance beyond the Bab el Oued, or Northern Gate. It is a grand structure, in the Romano-Byzantine style. This may be called the church of the sailors, as here are said masses especially for those lost at sea. To the brow of the promontory, every Sunday, the clergy march in procession, and perform funeral ceremonies above the vast grave yawning at their feet,— the sea. Upon a cross erected here I read this inscription: "Nôtre-Dame d'Afrique, S. Em. Le Cardinal Archbishop of Algiers and Carthage, Primate of Africa, has accorded in perpetuity an indulgence of one hundred days to those who will recite here a *pater* and an *ave* for the sailors who have perished in the sea, and those who have been in peril of death."

Out in this direction and above the city the views from the hill-tops are beautiful. I remember one sunset view I got from a high hill where the observatory is situated, and the wild nature of the walks along the hill-crests and side-hills, past Arab gardens and holy tombs. Perched upon the highest summit of the Sahel is the great fortification known as Fort de l'Empéreur, an ancient structure, first taken by the French when they attacked Algiers, and from which they held the Kasba and the city at their mercy.

Inside the city, again, one of the interesting places is the museum, in a building once the palace of the celebrated Mustapha Pacha. In its beautiful court we find some fascinating fragments of sculpture, including a gigantic statue of Neptune, a torso of Venus, a Faun and Hermaphrodite (all found in Africa), sculptured sarcophagi of the early years of Christianity, excellent mosaics, and a large library comprising many Arabian manuscripts. A grewsome thing shown here is a cast of Geronimo, an Algerian martyr of 1569. Geronimo (now Saint Geronimo) was an Arab boy who became converted to Christianity, and was martyred by the Algerines by being cast into a block of concrete and this block built into the wall of the fort. For three hundred years Geronimo lay there imbedded, and in 1853 the block was taken out and a plaster cast made of the mould in which he lay; and to-day you may see this memento of Moslem barbarity, in the shape of the cast of his skeleton, showing the distorted shape, and even the very cords with which he was bound.

Leaving the city by the southern gate, at several kilometers distance we find a delightful garden of all sorts of tropical plants and trees, called the Jardin d'Essai, — experimental garden. On the way we pass the broad parade-grounds where the soldiers manœuvre, and where the Arabs camp with their camels.

Above this is an Arab cemetery, which is much frequented on Fridays by the Moorish women. It contains the sacred tomb of Sidi Mohammed ben Abd-er-Rhaman bou Koberain, or the man with two tombs! The most attractive district of Algiers is that beyond the Porte d'Isly, called Mustafa Supérieur, where the houses of the European residents are mostly built, and where the numerous villas, many of them in the Moorish style, are surrounded with gardens. Here the summer palace of the governor-general is built, thoroughly Oriental in its architecture and tropical in its surroundings. Judging from descriptions, it is of the same style of the famous palace of Ghizireh, in Cairo, with its Moorish arches, fountains, corridors. We are constantly reminded of the farther East, in our wanderings through Southern Spain and Northern Africa, and ever turning back toward the Orient, — toward Cairo and Damascus, — for the types of architecture here presented.

CHAPTER X.

ALL ABOUT THE ALGERIANS.

T is the Professor this time who asks to be heard, and he says he cannot rest until he has disburdened himself of the information he has collected relative to the Algerian aborigines. It is so generally believed that the Moors and the French now occupy solely this great country, that the general reader may be astonished to learn that they are by no means in the majority. Fortunately for him, during his investigation he fell in with a little book in French which gave the history of these people, and without further prefatory explanation he herewith presents the gist of what he has translated.

The ancients have left us no trustworthy documents upon those people who first settled Algiers. According to Sallust, the northern part of Africa was first inhabited by two native races,—the Getules and the Libyans. Later, the Getules united with the Medes and Persians, and from the fusion of these two elements—one autochthon, the other Asiatic—sprang the Numidians, represented at the present day by the Berbers. This tradition from the annals of the Numidian kings easily accounts for facts being proven to-day. The dark type would represent the descendants of the Numidians, while the fair type, which is smaller in numbers, and is found especially in Morocco, would represent the posterity of the army of the Medes and the Persians. Tradition is also preserved of a Semitic migration from Canaan, supporting which is the fact that the Berbers have always had more affinity with the Semitic race and the Canaanites than with the Aryans.

If we compare the Berbers of Algeria with the Touaregs, it is easily seen that a relationship exists between them; they speak the same language, and their written characters are precisely the same as those in the rare inscriptions found in the mountains of Algeria and called Lybic. The origin of the ancestors of the Touaregs is evidently Oriental, from the Arabian peninsula on the borders of the Red Sea. Other invasions, either from Spain or from the Mediterranean coast, have without doubt co-operated in the formation of this Algerian people, the Berbers; but this ethnic contingent had not, before the Arabian conquest, furnished an element important enough to modify any of the essential traits in the characteristic physiognomy of the primitive populations of Algiers.

The monuments of large stones found in certain parts of Algiers are generally attributed to migration of Aryan origin; but this does not at all change the opinion concerning the little importance which has been assigned them. The small funeral monuments called *choucha* and *bazina*, which have been found in the mountains of Aures, are probably to be attributed to the autochthonic races; they were later imitated by the Numidian kings in the *Madghasen*, which is a sort of colossal *bazina*. The so-called "Tomb of the Christian" is an imitation of more recent date of these primitive tombs. All these monuments are built on the same plan, and are artificial hillocks covered with masonry, in shape a truncate cone, elliptical or circular at the base. Traces of the ancient worship of the Berbers have entirely disappeared. From the finding of Megalithic monuments in Spain, some writers have supposed an Aryan invasion through Europe, across the Straits of Gibraltar, after the death of Hercules; but this is not so probable as the invasion along the lines of the African coast. An invasion of Iberians (from Spain) is not very certain; and as to the Hellenes, they did not reach Algeria. The first people who in historic times came to settle in Algiers are the Phœnicians; but they came at first merely for trade, and had no perceptible effect upon the native types.

It was quite the opposite with the Moslem conquest; for from the first the Arabs imposed their religion and their language upon the greater number of the inhabitants. In the plains, their influence was such that it soon became impossible to distinguish the victors from the vanquished. The mountaineers resisted longer, but finally became zealous converts to Islamism.

In consequence of their invasion of Spain, and the struggles of all kinds they had to undergo, it was not long before the Arabs themselves disappeared from Algiers; but another invasion took place in the eleventh century, and after having ravaged the country, the greater part of these tribes settled in the southeastern part of Algeria, near the frontiers of Morocco, where they are now

ARAB WOMEN OF THE INTERIOR.

installed. A few even went into the interior of Morocco and helped by their arms to establish the dynasty which is reigning to-day. The French conquest is so recent that we can hardly estimate already the probable effect upon the natives of Algeria. Up to this time France has not been able to give much attention to the transformation of the people here; she has had too much to do in seeking to assure peace throughout the country: first, by means of arms; next, by the implantation of a European element large enough to insure respect from the vanquished. Thus by the side of the different races established in Algeria there is found by the union of the French with the other Europeans in the country, especially with the Spaniards and Italians, a new ethnical element whose representatives are already called by the distinctive term of Algerians. Though still few in numbers, this race has tendencies clearly enough defined to be noticed. The ethnographer finds the following element in Algeria: (1) the true Berbers, (2) the Arab Berbers, (3) the Arabs, (4) the Algerians, (5) the Jews. As to the *khouloughlis*, or half-breeds, children of Turks and native women, and the negroes, they are so few as scarcely to merit special mention. In round numbers, there may be a million Berbers, fifteen hundred thousand Arab Berbers, five hundred thousand Arabs, five hundred thousand Europeans, including the Algerians, and thirty-five thousand Jews. Most of the blacks are found in the oases, negroes from the Soudan; the *khouloughlis* are found in the cities, where there were formerly strong Turkish garrisons, and they occupy, as then, inferior governmental positions.

The dark type of the primitive population greatly resembles the Arab type, their distinctive features less accentuated in the Arab Berbers. Among the Berbers the bones of the skull are excessively hard and thick, and the children of their own accord practise striking the hardest objects with their heads. All natives wear the beard, though the head is completely shaven, with the exception of a tuft of hair on the very top. The members of certain brotherhoods often let this tuft grow until they can braid it. Circumcision is practised on all male children about the age of eleven years.

It is impossible to trace, even approximately, the physical characteristics of the new Algerian race, whose existence has but just commenced. The Berbers of the mountains inhabit houses grouped together into small villages, or peaks and hill-crests difficult of access. Their domestic animals are under the same roof, and separated from the family only by a low wall. No European could long endure the fatal emanations sent forth from these holes, where air and light enter only through one low door. The Berber costume consists of a long shirt, over which is the *burnous;* the legs, arms, and in summer the head, are generally bare. The women's costume consists simply of a woollen, shirt-like garment, belted around the waist. A handkerchief around the head, immense earrings, necklace, bracelets, and anklet rings, complete the attire. Men and women wear their clothes till they fall to pieces; sometimes they may patch them, but they never wash them! There is little variety to their food, their most common dish being the *cous-cous*, or lumps of flour cooked with the steam from the broth of meat, and strongly seasoned with butter or oil; add to this various fruits, such as dried grapes and figs, artichokes, beans, and peas. The Arab Berbers live sometimes in *gourbis*, or huts of branches, sometimes in tents made of camel's-hair.

The language has never been subject to literary culture; the only vestiges consist of translations of stories, of books on canonical law or on theology, written in Arabic. The Arab Berbers speak an Arab dialect, which contains but a very few native words. As a rule, the farther you go into the desert, the purer the Arabic spoken by the people. The Algerians, of course, speak the French, and generally without the slightest accent. Certain Arab words, as *razzia*, have even found a place in the Dictionary of the Academy (French). In Algeria, especially in Algiers (the city), they are quite active in scientific matters, but have produced very few works purely literary. The native Jews speak among themselves a corrupted Arabic, in which are mixed a considerable number of French words with Arabic inflections. In the province of Oran Spanish is generally spoken. The Berbers are revengeful, courageous, honest among themselves, though rapidly learning the Arab vice of cheating the stranger.

The social unit among the Berbers is the *kharrouaba*, or the members of one family, sometimes admitting others; and sometimes families and even villages unite in common interest, and thus a little republic may be formed. Each village is governed by an Amin, or mayor, who is assisted by a few of the chief men of the village. The *djemaa*, or municipal council, meets once a week to deliberate on the affairs of the community, all the males from the age of sixteen taking part. The Moslems here have no real clergy, and the mufti is more a magistrate than a priest. The caste of the *marabouts* has great religious influence, the quality of which is hereditary in the male line of all those who have led an exemplary religious life, or who have consecrated themselves exclusively to the defence of Islamism against the infidels. They used to live in convents. All do not know how to read, but to them is intrusted the education of the children. This consists in teaching them a few prayers, some chapters of the Koran, which they learn by heart, and a little reading and writing. Even the very "learned" *marabouts* never pass the line of instruction in European primary schools. Though polygamy is authorized by the Koran, the

MOORISH WOMEN AT HOME.

great majority of the Moslem population do not take advantage of it, simply because they cannot afford it, and for no other reason. The woman's position is practically that of a slave to her husband, and an ill-treated one at that. Sabbatical rest is unknown to the Moslems; the Friday service, at which they are obliged to assist, lasts but an hour, and they employ the rest of the day in their usual labors.

Of very warlike nature, the Arab Berbers, as well as the Arabs, seize upon the most trivial pretext to use their arms, and make a *razzia*, or pillage, of a neighboring territory.

A BRIDE BEING CONDUCTED TO HER HUSBAND'S HOUSE.

On the plains, life is comparatively easy, seed-time and harvest taking up about three months in the year, the rest being spent in idleness. The cattle, sheep, and horses require only to be led to fresh pastures, and are attended by the children. The women alone make the articles indispensable for all, such as the *haiks* and *burnouses*, the chief articles of clothing. The men make the wooden part of their ploughs, and plait baskets and ropes, which, with a two-edged pickaxe, made by a blacksmith, constitute their stock of agricultural tools. Earthen and wooden dishes, a pitcher and a kettle, comprise the kitchen and table utensils. The furniture consists of a few mats, a wooden chest, and sometimes a carpet.

In the cities, industries are more active and diverse; there are found especially potters, dyers, armorers, blacksmiths, tinkers, carpenters, tanners, and an incredible number of shoemakers, which seems surprising in a country where so many of the people go barefoot. The Arab woman of the town has greater freedom and less work than the country woman. Every Thursday the city women pass the afternoon at the Moorish baths, where they wear the most beautiful toilets. Friday they go to the cemetery, less in regard to the dead than to take the air in perfect liberty. This seems a strange place for a reunion, but is probably selected as being less exposed to the gaze of strangers. Their morals are said to be very loose.

Now, as to matters of history. After the destruction of Carthage, the Romans, little by little, extended their power over the whole of Algeria. In at first sustaining Masinissa against Syphax, they determined the creation of a Numidian kingdom, whose capital was Cirta (Constantine); numerous Roman colonies coming into Algeria precipitated the downfall of the Numidian dynasty. Jugurtha, frightened by the leading rôle taken by the Romans in his native land, sought to reconquer it, but was defeated and taken a captive to Rome about B. C. 106. Roman rule was not imposed without trouble, and the confidence of the natives was never won; so that when the Vandals came they made easy victories, and founded an empire which lasted from 423 to 583 A. D. This empire was destroyed by Belisarius, but the Byzantine occupation met with the greatest resistance from the natives, who were hardly subdued before the Arabs, in their turn, came to conquer northern Africa. It was in 646 that the Arabs arrived, and after a fierce struggle converted the Berbers to Islamism so complete that they were the most zealous invaders of Spain, for the propagation of the faith, in the year 711. But the Moslems were divided into different sects, and thus their conquest by the Turks, in 1515, was made quite easy. Turkish rule continued until the French occupation, in 1830; and as the tribes were allowed to be governed by their same *caids*, *beys*, and *aghas*, they accepted the change of government without great disquiet. But the French, unlike the Turks, desired a *territorial* conquest; hence the numerous and bloody revolts, only suppressed after years of bloodshed. To-day all the tribes have lost the freedom they enjoyed under the Turks; the natives are directly governed by agents in the pay of France, and their laws are greatly simplified. They have preserved all the practices of their religion, and the rare attempts at proselytism, either by the Protestants or Romanists, have been without result. The principal Arab settlements of those hordes who came here, driven by hunger from the shores of the Red Sea, have been in the southern parts of the province of Oran (Tlemcen) and in Morocco. The nomadic life has such a charm for those who have tried it in their youth, that it is impossible even to think of drawing the Arabs of the high plateaus, or of the Saharian region, from this mode of existence. Those long and constant peregrinations keep the body well and strong; and the heat of the sun, warming alike the body and brain, develops an exuberant imagination, which gives the nomads the highest value of their pleasures. They are like sailors in their love of the monotony of vast expanses and solitude. The Berbers are stupid, and have no literature; but the Arab Berbers enjoy the refined delights of the mind with a veritable dilettanteism, and listen for hours to the bards who traverse the land and charm by their endless recitals the long hours of their vacant, monotonous existence.

To conclude, and to summarize. The native races of Algeria possess qualities sufficient to bring them, in the near future, to a level with the average European, but they cannot be expected to attain this result by themselves; it is indispensable that they should be guided by a firm hand and intelligent direction. Notwithstanding the inherent difficulties of the conquest, France has already sought to ameliorate their material existence, and several years ago she began the work of moral and intellectual reform by the application of special laws for the instruction of the natives. Though the taking of Algiers dates from 1830, it is but just to recollect that the pacification of Kabylia was not completed until 1860, and there have been serious revolts as late as 1871.

THE ARAB'S SONG OF VICTORY.

France has undertaken a great work, and she has shown her fitness for the task of civilizing all Northern Africa. Her Algerian colony, in truth, is vastly better governed than France herself.

Now, since our readers have been so patient with us as to read this description of the Berbers, we will treat them to a story which we find in a book of adventures in Algiers. It is an amusing account of how a conceited young lion came to grief.

THE CONCEITED YOUNG LION.

Among the lords of Mount Aures there once lived and loved a lioness, who, though long wedded, had never yet become a mother. But the event so devoutly prayed for was at length realized, and one morning's sun, as it poured upon the broad roof of the cedar and lotus, and glinted down among grape-vines and olives, at last played upon and brightened one tawny cub, that nestled in its warm bed of leaves beneath. With long walks and simple diet the lioness strengthened her infant's frame, and with good counsel she fortified his understanding. Above all things she warned him to beware of the seed of the woman.

As the weeks fled by, the strength of the young lion increased. His limbs developed their muscles, his mane came out little by little, and his voice, at first so weak, and whining like a girl's, became so valorous that the flocks when they heard it kicked up their heels and scampered to the *douars*. One day he came to his mother, saying,—

"Now I am strong and courageous; the seed of the woman I can hold down with one paw. I think I will go out and teach him obedience."

The mother, frightened at this foolhardy bravery, endeavored to dissuade him from the attempt; but all her efforts were unheeded, or answered only by a pettish growl. Not being able to turn his determination, she renewed her prudent counsels, and with a fond lick or two of her caressing tongue gave him to the charge of Allah and the Prophet. The young lion bounded bravely out of the jungle that had cradled his cubbish hours, and resolutely gained the ridge of the mountains. For a long time he walked boldly on, without seeing anything worthy his steel. Fox and stag and light gazelle vanished as he came, his very voice stilled the forest around him, and his young heart swelled high with triumph.

Presently he saw a bull on one of the plains below him, his horns like pine-trees, his eyes darting red fire, his tail swinging back and forth like a thrasher's flail, and his hoofs tearing the sod from the earth and scattering it like hail.

"Ha, ha!" said the young lion, "there is a warlike creature, that might well be called the seed of the woman, that rules the earth. That is my enemy; I will march at him."

He walked up with a fierce air to the bull, and in a tone of great emphasis demanded, "Are you the seed of the woman?"

The bull dropped his tail and replied: —

"My dear friend, you are foolish. The courage that God has given to the seed of the woman he has granted to no other living creature. Do you know how he treats me and my race? He puts yokes over our necks and makes us do his work. If we are idle he beats us with goads; and when too old to act longer as his servants, he slays us and divides our flesh to feed his wives and children."

THE CONCEITED YOUNG LION.

The lion listened to this story; a look of sage wonder mantled his countenance, and he continued his course. After walking a little while, he presently encountered face to face a camel, that was pasturing on a delicate patch of thistles.

"This time I have hit it," said the lion to himself; then to the camel he said, "Sirrah, are you the seed of the woman?"

The camel laughed outright as he tilted up his long neck from the thistle-bed. "You have n't hit it at all, Master Lion, though you are so wise. What do you want of the seed of the woman? If you will heed the advice of a stranger who has known him a long while, you will keep the greatest distance from him you can. Look at me. Are you able to bend my knees to the earth, to bind pack after pack on my back, and then mounting yourself on the top of all, to guide me and drive me over the desert? That is what the person you seek does to me every day; and if he chooses to cut my stomach open to find water for his children, I cannot resist. Now, then, do you fancy the acquaintance? If so, you have only to go ahead, and you will find him."

"You are a poltroon, you cowardly camel!" retorted the lion, in a disdainful tone. "Your old woman's tales and the stories of the bull only enter one ear to go out the other; I will continue my road."

In a few minutes he saw a horse coursing the fields like the wind; his neigh was music on the air, and his breath was white like smoke.

"Holloa!" called the lion from afar. "I am looking for the son of the woman; are you not he?"

"Are you speaking to me?" said the horse.

"Who else is there to speak to?"

"Then go somewhere else with your jokes, for I have never found any joking in connection with that name. The son of the woman, prithee! he has saddled and bridled me, though I am swift on the foot, and curbs me to his will."

"Indeed!" said the lion, as his eyes began to open visibly.

"Indeed, it is true; and then he sits on my back, and, carry him fast as I may, he drives the spurs into my side until the sands are dotted with my blood."

"Oh!" said the lion, in a voice that made the horse take to his heels. The perspiration started under his mane, and he began to think he had not looked before he had leaped. However, it was too late to doubt, and he pushed on.

The plain was passed, and a forest rose before him on the side of a purling brook, and from time to time, like the call of a bell-bird, he heard the clear sound of a woodman's axe. Entering the woods, guided by the noise, he saw before him the wood-chopper.

"This fluttering jay-bird may tell me something about what I am seeking," muttered the lion, "though he is so tattered and poor he may not even have heard of the great ones of the earth. God help you, my poor creature! I have been all day hunting after the seed of the woman; can you tell me where I must go to find him?"

"Good gracious! most noble sir, he's not hard getting at; I'll go and fetch him. But please, sir, while I am gone, this log I am splitting won't stay open unless you will hold it for me. Just put your paw in this crack; I won't be gone a minute."

The lion with a gracious condescension inserted his paw in the crevice, when the wily woodman knocked away the wedge that held it open, and the log, springing together, held the lion's paw with a grip like a vise. He struggled and growled in vain. The woodman then cut a dozen stout cudgels, and taking the lion by the tail with one hand, administered with the other such an awful bastinado that the poor creature's back was beaten softer than his belly. At length, when strength and sticks were all worn out, he released his prisoner by driving in another wedge, telling him to go home and relate to his family that if they would all come there, the seed of the woman would give them the same lesson. The poor lion took his way home, half dead with shame and pain, and limping like a rabbit. The mother was out watching for the return of her hopeful, and when she saw him coming in this wretched plight she roared with horror and indignation, and bitterly reproached him for his folly. She then led him in, and having put him on her best bed, she licked his wounds and administered to him all the care that art and love could suggest. The young lion then told over his adventures.

"THE LIONS BEGAN TO ARRIVE."

The mother said, "Do you remain here quietly. I will summon all the lions of the mountain, and leading them myself, I will avenge your insults, my poor child." And great tears of sympathy and anger rolled down her hairy cheeks while speaking.

She then went out and roused all the forces of the mountain, and presently with the rising sun the lions began to arrive, trooping past like kings. Pointing out the formidable squadron to her son, she said, "Do you think they can avenge you?"

"Yes, certainly; but I would rather do it myself."

"Rise and march with us, then," said the proud mother; and the young lion rose and led the van. The terrible band then started for the forest by the purling brook. As it came, terrified Nature fled away. The wood-chopper, seeing its approach, cried out, —

"I am a miserable sinner; this day will I see the prophet!" Then recovering himself a little, he hugged a big tree and shinned up to the top.

The leonine army came to the foot of the tree; but alas! their enemy was at the top and they at the bottom, and there was no manœuvre in their system of warfare adapted for such a position. They held a council of war. The young lion was among the speakers, and proposed the following plan: —

"I will stand against the tree; let another of you mount my shoulders.

taking the same position, and then another and another, until we form a ladder that will reach the wretch and drag him down."

This counsel was considered good, and forthwith a pyramid of lions might have been seen climbing up the side of the tree, one above another, and gradually approaching the refugee. The topmost round of the ladder was made, and the wood-cutter almost reached, when he cried out in a loud voice, —

"Hold on till I cut a cudgel and give that fellow at the bottom another drubbing!"

The sound of this voice, so dreadful, but above all the remembrance of the cudgelling he had received, so frightened the young lion that was at the bottom of the pyramid, that he jumped out from under his comrades, and took to his heels with surprising agility. The ladder of lions, suddenly deprived of its support, came tumbling to the ground with a great crash. They fell from such a prodigious height that those not killed were stunned and wounded, and all lay moaning in a heap. Then the wood-cutter slipped down and seized his axe. He killed all those that were wounded, and stripping the skins from them all, he gayly marched to his *douar*, the richest man from Cairo to Timbuctoo.

CHAPTER XI.

A LION-HUNT IN THE AURES MOUNTAINS.

N going from Algiers to Constantine you have a taste of North African quality in the great variety of scene and the glimpses into history afforded by the towns along the line. Though much of the route is most monotonous, yet there are grand mountains, gloomy gorges and ravines where yet lurk the lion and the panther. Such gorges are the Portes de Fer, near the station of Sidi Brahem. Many of the towns have mournful memories of the native revolts of 1871, such as that of Palaestro, a village seventy-seven kilometers from Algiers, whose population of Tyrolese, French, and Spanish immigrants was massacred in a manner peculiarly atrocious. At two hundred and ninety-four kilometers from Algiers we reach Setif, a very ancient city, known to the Romans as Sitifi Colonia, a flourishing colony in the Middle Ages. Many Roman remains may still be seen here.

A great future is predicted for Setif, as it is high and healthy, and is geographically well situated, especially with reference to the railway lines from the ports Bougie and Djigelli. The port of Bougie, by the way, is the place that gave the name to the French candle; and who does not remember the frequent recurrence of the everlasting *bougie, un franc*, in his hotel bill? Not far from the station of Telegma, about forty kilometers from Constantine, the most beautiful remains of Roman art in Africa were discovered in

1878, consisting of buildings once belonging to the celebrated Roman, Pompeianus, pro-consul of Africa in the reign of Honorius. The mosaic floors are supposed to be of the first or second century, and represent domestic and hunting scenes with great beauty and fidelity.

The objective point of this long railroad ride is the famous city of Constantine, declared to be the most picturesque, as to its natural situation, in the world. It covers the summit platform of a rock plateau square in shape, with perpendicular sides rising nearly one thousand feet, in places, above the river Roummel, which flows around it on the north and east. This river, flowing through its cañon walls, is spanned by four natural bridges of rock, one of which supports the bridge by which the city is reached, El Kantara. Constantine was a sister city of Carthage, whose king at one time, Narva (who reigned about 230 B. C.), was married to a sister of Hannibal. It was then known as Cirta, and the capital of Numidia, until its name was changed to Constantine, about the year 313.

It is a city celebrated in ecclesiastical history also, and connected with the great Saint Augustine and the early Christian bishops of Africa. To the student of ecclesiastical history, especially that period when Africa and Egypt were brought under the dominion of the Church, how fascinating must this city appear! Relics of Romans, Churchmen, Arabs, Vandals, are found here on every side. The last of the Deys here built a magnificent palace that the world may well come to now, and gaze at in wonder. But this city, this ancient capital, came under French rule in 1837, and the last of those miserable Moors and Turks, so long in power, were banished from the country.

I have not time to describe its interesting features, but the word of a traveller may be taken that it is worth a long, long journey to see. Monuments with Latin inscriptions may be found on every hand, and a Roman aqueduct, repaired, brings water to the city.

From Constantine — or rather from the port of Philippeville, north of it — a railroad drops southwardly into the desert. At

A LION AND A LIONESS.

present you can go no farther than Biskra, two hundred and thirty kilometers, whence roads or trails branch out into the unknown. From Batna, about midway this journey, one may reach the little-known Aures Mountains, where reside people supposed to be descended from mixed Romans, Byzantines, and Vandals, and whose women are said to be among the handsomest in the world.

Other pursuits than agriculture draw hither many strangers, especially the pursuit of sport; but if the farmers' rewards are meagre, so are the returns of the sportsmen. The season for shooting lasts from September to February, and, as in France and all her colonial possessions, one must have a *permis de chasse*. Partridges, snipe, duck, and woodcock are sometimes found, but not in abundance. Yet there are many wild animals remaining in this country, where "Gerard the Lion-killer" found such sport in his time. In the twelve years between 1873 and 1884, inclusive, above thirty thousand wild animals were killed, for which rewards were paid, including one hundred and eighty-one lions and a thousand panthers.

The rarest sport is that of falconry, which certain of the Arabs indulge in at the south. It is said that the art of training falcons is hereditary, and it requires great skill and patience. The hawks are snared and hooded, and perched upon their master's shoulders, which are protected by strips of leather. They are fed only by their captors, and when they have become attached to them, after two months or so, they are taken to the field, hooded, and the hood removed only when the quarry is in sight, at which they fiercely dash. Falconry is carried on only by the chiefs, or Arabs of high caste, and the poor are not permitted to indulge in it. The falcon is caught in a net, beneath which is a partridge or a hare. It is kept on a perch stuffed with hair, and subdued by being deprived of light and food for several days.

Perhaps the most comical yet savage people we saw, were the porcupine-hunters, who prowled about the mountains armed with clubs. They take with them a boy clad in skins, who looks like a naked human spider, and who crawls into the hole after the porcupine, pulling him out for the men to despatch with their clubs; after which they have a great feast.

But what interested our party most, when we reached the region of the Aures Mountains, was that we were now on the old hunting-ground of "Gerard the Lion-killer," who killed so many lions some forty years ago. His headquarters were about Guelma, in the province of Constantine and the country of the Ouled Hamza. The Mahouna, he says, was the pleasure-garden of the lions.

Between Constantine and Batna there may be seen the ruined minaret of an old convent-mosque, called Juna-el-Bechira, which has a most tragic history. For tradition says that the entire faculty of this old convent-college, some forty in number, were devoured by lions. One after another, sometimes in the garden, sometimes at the spring where they went for water, the monks were pounced upon and carried away by the king of beasts, until the two or three remaining fled in terror from the place. We did not have the opportunity for a lion-hunt, because the few lions remaining are so shy that even the Arabs seldom see them; but as we are on the ground of some of the great Gerard's famous exploits, what can we do better than let him tell one of his stories in his own modest language?

THE LION-KILLER'S STORY.

"On the desert, when an Arab, the owner of a large tent, marries a wife, he bids all the world to the wedding, and the guests go to the bride's tent to conduct her to her new home. The girl is carried in a palanquin, and the guests march by her side, making the night gay with music and a general fusillade.

"But as all men do not herd the same number of cattle, so all marriages are not alike. If one is honored by a great cortège, and gay cavaliers, rich in trappings and well-earned name, caracole by the side of the future spouse, another groom may not have the means even to pay the fiddler who makes the music. Smail, a young warrior of our tribe, belonged to this latter class, and his last crown had been spent to endow the bride. His retinue was confined to his near relatives, and on the auspicious day he came on foot to the tent of his future father-in-law, like a very peasant. Here the brave couple and their friends feasted on mutton and *couscousson;* and when the repast was done they fired away with powder and ball, taking care to reserve enough to use, in case of need, on their way home.

"The *douar* of the husband was only a league and a half away. It was a bright moonlight evening, and the party numbered nine guns; what was there to make them afraid? But is it not when the tent is gayest, that trouble draws the curtain and steps in at the door? Truly the good people were gay, and as they returned, in merry mood, they sang as they frolicked over the sand. Smail walked at the head of the procession with his dark-eyed wife, and his head was bent and his voice was low, whispering soft promises of the pleasures that were awaiting them under his tent. His friends were behind, discreetly loitering at a little distance, and from time to time their guns awoke the echoes among the distant hills. But on a sudden the Devil, who had not been bidden to the wedding, presented himself before them in the shape of an enormous lion, and crouched down in the very path of the procession!

"What was to be done? They were half-way between the two *douars*, and it was as dangerous to return as to advance. The occasion to win the devotion of his wife forever was too tempting for Smail to allow it to pass. The guns were all loaded with ball, the bride was placed in the middle of a hollow square formed by the guests, — brave men all, — and the escort marched on, led by the bridegroom. They came to within thirty paces of the lion, and yet he moved not. Smail ordered the party to halt, and then saying to his wife, 'Judge if you have married a man or not,' he walked straight up to the wild beast, summoning him in a loud voice to clear the road. At twenty paces the lion raised its monstrous head and prepared to spring. Smail, in spite of the cries of his wife and the entreaties of his friends, who counselled a retreat, bent one knee to the earth, took aim, and fired. The lion, wounded by the shot, sprang on the husband, hurled him to the earth, tore him in pieces in the twinkling of an eye, and then charged the group, in the middle of which stood the bride.

"'Let no man fire,' shouted the father of Smail, 'until he is within gun's length!'

"But where is the man who is strong enough at heart to await, with firm foot and steady hand, this thunderbolt of hell which is called a lion, when with flowing mane, blazing eye, and open mouth he charges on him with immense bounds? All fired at once, without regarding whither their balls went, and the lion fell upon the group, dashing them hither and thither, breaking the bones and tearing the flesh of all he found within reach. Nevertheless, some escaped, carrying with them the bride half dead with terror. A moment more, and the lion was after them; there was no refuge and no defence, and the wounded

AN OASIS APPEARING IN A MIRAGE TO TRAVELLERS IN THE DESERT.

beast seized and tore to pieces one after another, until but one was left of the party. He reached the foot of a steep rock, on which he placed the woman, and then began climbing up after her. He had already reached twice the height of a horseman, when the lion gained the rock as furious as ever. With a single

A MOUNTAIN PASS IN TUNIS.

bound he seized the unfortunate man by the leg and dragged him backward to the ground, while the woman reached the summit of the rock, from whose inaccessible height she watched the horrid spectacle, — the death-agony of the last of her defenders. After one or two unsuccessful bounds the lion returned to the dead body of his last victim, and commenced mangling and tearing it in small pieces, in revenge for the loss of the poor wife that looked down at him from above. The rest of the night passed slowly to the lonely woman. When the morning dawned, the lion retired to the mountain; but he departed reluctantly, and not without stopping and returning more than once, with a covetous whine, for the cowering bride he had left behind. Shortly after he had gone, a group of horsemen appeared on the plain. The stricken bride, without any voice to call, waved her bridal veil as a signal of distress. They came to her at a gallop, and carried her to her father's tent, where she died the next night at the hour of the wedding."

That was the Arab's story; but I will omit the exclamations, taunts, and reproaches, that were hurled at the murderer after it was finished. One after another they told their different tales, and it was not till late that the party broke up, — the Arabs to return to their tents, with many God's blessings for my success, and I to remain on the watch for the lion, with a native corporal of the spahis, whose brother was a sheik of this country.

The path on which we were lying ascended the steep hillside, from a densely wooded ravine where the lion kept himself by day, to the high plateau on which the Arabs dwelt. At about one o'clock in the morning Saadi-bou-Nar, but little accustomed to these night-watches, pleaded guilty to being very sleepy, and stretched himself out behind me and slept most soundly.

Up to this time the heavens had been serene and the moon clear; but soon clouds gathered in the west and came scudding past before a warm, sultry wind, the sky was overcast, the moon was gone, and the thunder rolled around us in heavy peals, announcing a coming tempest. Then the rain fell in torrents, and drenching my companion, he awoke, and we consulted for a moment about returning to the *douar*. But while we were talking, an Arab from the camp called out, "Beware! the lion will come with the storm!"

This decided me to remain at my post, and I covered the locks of my gun with the skirts of my coat. Soon the rain ceased, like all rains that accompany a thunder-gust, and we only saw its passage by the lightning that tracked the distant horizon; and the moon, more brilliant than ever, came in and out from the fleecy clouds overhead. I took advantage of every one of these short instants of clear sky to survey the country about me, and to penetrate with a glance each clump of trees or fallen log; and it was in one of these brief moments that, all of a sudden, I thought I saw a lion. I waited breathless till the moon came out again. Yes, *it was surely a lion*, standing motionless only a few paces from the camp! Accustomed to see fires lighted at every tent, to hear a hundred dogs barking in terror, and to see the men of the camp hurling lighted brands at him, he without doubt was at loss to explain the rather suspicious silence that reigned around him. While I was turning slowly around, in order to take better aim without being seen by the animal, a cloud shut out

MEDJERDAB, THE MOST IMPORTANT RIVER IN TUNIS.

the moon. But at last the scud passed, and the moonlight, dearer to me than the most beautiful sunshine, illuminated the picture, and again showed me the lion still standing in the same place. I saw him the better as he was so much raised above me, and he loomed up proudly magnificent, standing as he was in majestic repose, with his head high in air, and his flowing mane undulating in the wind and falling to his knees. It was a black lion, of noble form and the largest size. As he presented his side to me, I aimed just behind his shoulder, and fired. I heard a fierce roar of mingled pain and rage echoing up the hills with the report of the gun, and then from under the smoke I *saw the lion bounding upon me!*

Saadi-bou-Nar, roused the second time that night from his slumber, sprang to his gun, and was about to fire over my shoulder. With a motion of my arm I pushed aside the barrel of his gun, and when the beast, still roaring furiously, was within three steps of me, I fired my second barrel directly into his breast.

13

Before I could seize my companion's gun the lion rolled at my feet, bathing them in the blood that leaped in torrents from his throat! He had fallen dead so near me that I could have touched him from where I stood.

At the first moment I thought I was dreaming, and that it was impossible that the huge bulk which lay motionless before me was the same animal which, endowed with superhuman strength, and vomiting peals of thunder, was just before leaping through the air. But the cries of Saadi-bou-Nar, calling the Arabs to the scene, proved to me that it was no dream. I cannot explain the reason; but the death of the lion did not give me the same pleasure as that of my first victim; but how could it be otherwise?

In looking for my balls, I found the first one, the one that had not killed, just behind the shoulder, where I had intended it to hit; and the second, that had been fired in haste, and almost at hazard, had been the one that was mortal. From this moment I learned that it does not suffice to aim correctly in order to kill a lion, and that

A MOSQUE IN TUNIS.

it is a feat infinitely more serious than I had at first supposed. But slowly my preoccupation became dissipated, and little by little, as I contemplated the lordly grace of my victim, and heard the reports of musketry carrying the fame of my victory from camp to camp, I became less thoughtful, and drank with pleasure the intoxicating cup of success.

CHAPTER XII.

TUNIS, CARTHAGE, AND THE GREAT DESERT.

E lingered long, and we reverently searched for some traces of the great lion-killer; the Professor was also interested in the ethnology of the region, and would gladly have remained a month. There was yet ahead of us, however, a city of fame, Tunis, and another in ruins, Carthage, which all of us were impatient to behold.

Tunis, although a recent acquisition of the French, is certainly a portion of their possessions, — geographically a portion of Algiers, and united with all French Africa by the great railroad I have mentioned. The Gulf of Tunis early attracted the attention of the Phœnician engagers, and here Carthage was founded, about 850 B.C. The city of Tunis occupies a position between the lakes, or lagoons, while the ancient Carthage was nearer the open gulf. Of its situation an English artist writes: —

"No words can do it justice. The great bay is almost land-locked; billowy peaks to the east; in the dim distance the blue hills of the Laghouan range, the mountains that look down upon the far-famed city of Kairwan; directly in front the white houses of the Goletta, — the present harbor of Tunis; away to the west the stony amphitheatre, rich with the memories of two thousand years, where once stood Carthage, the very spot from which Dido looked with longing eyes upon the white sails of her hero-lover as they floated over this lovely bay; and beyond Carthage, with its great college of St. Louis now dominating the spot, was the lofty peak on the edge of which is built the walled Arab town of Sidi bou Said. Everywhere there are fine hills in graceful outline sweeping down to the blue waters of the gulf, and everywhere strange tropical trees, lofty date-palms, and straggling prickly-pear.

"I know of no city except Constantinople that occupies a site which can be compared with this. Even that of Ephesus is inferior in splendor, if not in interest. The great city occupied an amphitheatre sloping gently down to the edge of the gulf." Such is the situation of Carthage. But, *Delendo est Carthago.* "The impression to-day is one of intense disappointment. The Roman wish has been fulfilled, and of the once glorious Carthage not one stone remains standing above ground.

"The whole site of the city is strewn with the broken fragments of pottery, mosaics, sculptures, marbles, pillars, tiles. Everywhere, too, huge fallen masses of masonry are lying prone upon the earth. The site of Dido's palace is shown, and beyond the extensive cisterns vast subterranean structures with heavy vaulted roofs. In every case the masonry is of the most substantial character, showing how well the Phœnicians did their work."

A VIEW OF THE NEW PORTION OF BISKRA.

There is a rich field for excavation here. "Three towns lie atop each other, one Punic, one Roman, and the last Byzantine." Tunis, now the chief city of this great gulf, "grew out of the ashes of the Roman colony, and received its autonomy only with Islam. The Arabs destroyed all evidences of Christian culture, overthrew the temples, and with the fragments built their own mosques and palaces."

A CAMPING-PLACE IN SIGHT OF BISKRA.

Though Tunis has been declared more Oriental than the Orient, than even Cairo and Damascus, yet the inter-communication afforded by the railroad has robbed it somewhat of its very distinctive character. Its bazaars may be more richly furnished than those of Algiers and Tlemcen, but not sufficiently to merit further description.

Americans should not forget that it was at Tunis that John Howard Payne, author of "Home, Sweet Home," was at one time consul for our government. Here he died, and here lay buried many years, until his remains were taken to the United States several years ago, at the expense of Mr. Corcoran, of Washington.

Leaving Tunis, now, let us make a journey toward and into the Great Desert.

The finest oases are said to be south of Tunis, toward Tripoli, such as Sfax and Gabes, some of which contain from two to three hundred thousand palm-trees. In most of the oases the palm-groves are planted many feet below the general surface of the desert, in the aquiferous sand beneath the surface-crust of gypsum, where the semi-subterranean streams alone are found in circulation. Thus a mound of verdure may sometimes be seen rising dome-shaped above the sands, without any visible trunks to the trees.

These oases, of course, are the result of springs of water, of streams that gush out from subterranean sources. While writing of this subject, it may be as well to sketch the natural divisions of North Africa in general, to show how climate is modified by the surface configuration. There are three generally accepted divisions: First, that littoral strip of territory called the Tell, consisting of fairly fertile cultivated land extending from the coast to the mountains and high plateaus, and varying from fifty to one hundred miles in width. The Atlas Mountains cross the territory with a general trend from southeast to northwest; from Cape Nun, on the Atlantic (Morocco), to Tunis, on the Mediterranean. They approach within thirty miles of the city of Algiers, and between their lateral ridges are fertile valleys, like the Metidja. South of the mountains and plateaus begins the Sahara, which may occupy as vast a territory as the geographers will admit. The scheme of converting the Sahara into an inland sea has been discussed; but I think it is now abandoned as not feasible, or not likely to be of benefit if it were so converted.

During our journey thither we met with clouds of locusts, which spread over the land, devouring every green thing. These locusts have been a great scourge to Algiers. The following account may give some idea of their ravages.

"In May, 1844, they appeared in such numbers that the richest agricultural districts were made deserts. The indolence of the natives and the unsettled condition of the country were against any systematic efforts to exterminate the little pests. Moreover, the superstitious natives charged the Christian conquerors with conjuring the evil one, and rebellions were the result.

"In March, 1885, the locusts again made their appearance. Two months later the districts Altmale, Bou-Saada, Boghar, Chellala, and Laghouat were overrun, and the fields stripped of every kind of growth. In the spring of 1886 the locusts reappeared. This year the Sirocco — that terrible hot wave of the desert — swept over Algiers with unusual fierceness, charged with the sand of the great Sahara, and with millions and millions of locusts. In a few days the whole country was covered with these pests. Their ravages are terrible. The cattle, of which the colony contained sixteen million, are dying for want of nourishment, and a famine is threatening the European colonists. The government employs thousands of natives and all the available troops in a systematic effort to destroy the voracious little insects.

"Various devices are resorted to. Two such are most in favor, — the *melnafas*, and the *appareils cypriotes*. The former consists of cotton or woollen cloth of a very rough surface, which is spread over the ground. The locusts are caught in the coating, are shaken together and turned into deep ditches or stamped to death. The *appareils cypriotes* are sheets of muslin about two hundred feet long and three feet wide, stretched over frames and placed upright along the path of the invaders. It is the habit of the locust not to turn in its progress, but to endeavor to surmount every obstacle in its way. It will try to climb the cloth, which is beaten by sticks. The insects fall to the ground, are swept together and destroyed. The artillery also fires heavy charges of blank cartridges into the swarms, the cavalry is employed to stamp the insects into the ground, and the native troops are not furnished with rations of meat, in order to stimulate their appetite for the great national dish, — stewed locusts, broiled locusts, and locust raw.

MOSQUE OF SIDI BEN FERDHA, BISKRA.

"It is an ancient and sacred custom of the natives to eat these insects. Tradition has it that at the first appearance of the locusts Mahomet instructed his disciples not to destroy them. But one day the great prophet noticed on the wings of one of these insects an inscription in Hebrew characters, saying: 'We are the soldiers of God ; we lay ninety-nine eggs. Whenever we shall lay one hundred, the universe will have been devoured by us.' Horrified at this sacrilege, the prophet straightway interviewed the Lord, and received the order that as a punishment of the locusts the faithful should kill and eat them. That the natives highly relish the dish appears from the saying: 'Next to the date the locust is the sweetest morsel.' The Koran prohibits the flesh of animals not born; but the Mahometan doctors of law, as become wise and dutiful guardians of their flocks, denied that locusts were fish, that as such the common people might eat them, while the men in holy order should deny themselves this sweet morsel in order to avoid the temptation to gorge themselves."

THE NATIVE QUARTER OF BISKRA.

For the finest oases we must push on to Biskra, the terminal of the railroad projected in this direction. Biskra is a charming desert town, composed mainly of mud buildings, with a great palm-grove near and around it. The oasis of Biskra is said to contain one hundred thousand palm-trees; and as it is abundantly supplied with water from running streams and artesian wells, it has smiling

MOSQUE OF SIDI MOHHAMMED, AT BISKRA.

fields and luxuriant gardens. Its climate is tropical, except during the winter months, and the air is pure and dry. Biskra, the "Queen of the Libyan," is the northernmost of that archipelago of oases that traverse the great sea of the desert.

But I should not neglect to mention yet another village of the Libyan archipelago, about twelve or fifteen miles from Biskra, called Okba. Here also are beautiful oases, and here is probably the "oldest Mahometan monument in Africa,"— the Mosque of Sidi Okba, an Arabian warrior who is said to have conquered this country in the sixtieth year of the Hegira; and this memorial mosque is dated from the early years of the eighth century. It is about one hundred feet long, this primitive building, and from its minaret is a most magnificent view of the surrounding country. An inscription here, in Cufic characters, is said to be "perhaps the oldest Arabian inscription in the world," and reads: "This is the tomb of Okba, son of Nafa. May God have mercy upon him." He and some three hundred of his men were massacred here by the Berbers, in the year of our era 882.

A MOSQUE IN THE SAHARA DESERT.

A discovery of much archæological interest was recently made in the Algerian Sahara. M. Tarry, who has been carrying on work in connection with the proposed Trans-Sahara railroad, having noticed a mound of sand in the neighborhood of Wargal, had the sand dug up, and discovered the top of a dome. This naturally aroused his interest, and getting his Arabs to dig still deeper, he found underneath the dome a square tower, then a platform of masonry, and finally a complete mosque. Continuing the excavations, M. Tarry soon unearthed seven houses in perfect preservation, and came upon a subterranean watercourse. At the last news nine houses had been disinterred, and M. Tarry was getting additional assistance to clear out the precious watercourse, which he describes as sufficient to irrigate a small forest of palms. It is well known that the Sahara was at one time much more populated than it is now, and its trade much more extensive; but no one seems to have supposed that cities had been buried under its sands, at least so recently as since the introduction of Mahometanism.

One day, while we were sitting under a palm-tree at Biskra, the Doctor read to us the charming Arab story of Aïcha, from that delightful book of the Lion-killers; and as it pleased us then, perhaps it may also please the readers of our own adventure; so here it is. An Arab is the narrator of the story, telling it to a stranger who had chanced to visit his *douar*.

AÏCHA, THE LION'S LOVE.

Once upon a time, and a hundred years or more before I saw the light of the sun, there lived a maiden in our tribe that made famous the name of Aïcha. This maiden was very proud; not that she was richer than the other girls of the tribe, for her father had nothing but his tent, his gun, and his horse; but she was beautiful as a shady tree, and from her beauty was born her pride.

One day, while she was out cutting wood in a forest, she saw a large lion on a rock above her. At first he seemed not to notice her, but soon discovered her presence. Her only weapon was a little hatchet; but this, she knew, was of little account, for had she been armed like a mailed knight she would never have dared to attack, or defend herself from, so fierce an enemy. Her limbs sank beneath her; she tried to call out, but her voice fell to a whisper, and the lion seemed to beckon her to follow him, that he might devour her in some secret and hidden retreat. The damsel stood in trembling terror, waiting for the king of beasts to lead her wherever he would; but what was her astonishment when she saw him come down from the rock with the best smile he could assume on his wrinkled face, and make such a bow as only lions can make.

Then she crossed her hands on her breast, and said, "Seignior, what dost thou command thy humble servant to do?"

Then answered the lion: "When one is as beautiful as you are, Aïcha, one is no longer a servant, but a queen."

As may be imagined, Aïcha was as much astonished at the unaccustomed sweetness of his voice, as pleased that so great and beautiful a lion, and one whom she had never met before, should be acquainted with her name.

"Who told you," she inquired, "that my name was Aïcha?"

"The wind, that is in love with you, and that is fragrant with roses after it has toyed with your hair, whispers 'Aïcha;' the water, that bathes your feet, and then runs past my grotto, doth murmur 'Aïcha;' the birds, that, hearing you sing become jealous and die of shame, all the while sing of 'Aïcha,' only 'Aïcha.'"

The young girl, blushing with pleasure, made believe pull down her *haik* over her face, but only pushed it farther back, that the lion might see the better. He had before hesitated to approach very near her, but now advanced, only to see her face grow white with terror at the near approach of his huge lips. In a tone that was both anxious and fondly caressing, he said, "What is the matter, Aïcha?"

The maiden felt moved to say, "I am afraid of thee;" but did not dare to do so, and concealed her feelings by saying, "The Touaregs are near us, and I am afraid of them."

At this the lion's mouth spread into a smile, and he proudly replied: "Am I not with you, Aïcha? And when I am near you need fear nothing."

"But I will not always have thee with me," said Aïcha; "it is a great way from here to my father's tent, and it is growing late."

"But I will gladly see you home," gallantly replied the lion. Taken so by surprise, what could the poor girl do but accept. The lion walked to her side, and offered her his mane. She wound her fair hand in his tawny locks, and with her arm resting on his neck as it would have rested on the shoulder of her lover, the twain, each so beautiful, and yet so opposite in their different perfections, walked together toward the *douar* of the tribe. In the road they met dark-eyed gazelles that fled from them, and hyenas that crouched to the earth, and men and women that prostrated themselves as to a god. But the lion said to the gazelles, "Do not run away," and to the hyenas, "Be not afraid," and to the men and women, "Rise up, for by the grace of this young girl, who is my own true love, I will do you no harm." Then, at the royal word, the gazelles wheeled in their swift flight, the fierce hyenas raised their ugly faces, the men and women rose to their feet, and they all asked: "What is the meaning of this beautiful scene? Do the lion and the girl go together to worship at the tomb of the prophet in Mecca?"

Thus they walked, down through the gum-dropping forest, and over the blossom-scented field, until they came to the *douar*, and the white tent of Aïcha's father rose to sight. Here the lion paused, and with all the grace of a royal courtier he asked the maiden's permission to kiss her.

She proffered her warm and blushing cheek, and the lion, with his great tongue, licked the red lips of Aïcha. He then bowed her farewell, and sat himself down to watch and make sure that she reached her tent in safety. The girl turned her head three or four times, in the short walk before her, and she saw the lion always watching her from the same place, until she entered the tent.

"Ah! at last you have come," said her father.

The girl smiled.

"I feared you had met with some unpleasant encounter in the woods."

The girl smiled again.

"But since you are here, it is a proof that you have not been troubled."

"Indeed, my father, I have had a very pleasant encounter; that is, if you call a lion a pleasant person to meet."

Notwithstanding the ordinary impassibility of the Arab, the old man turned pale.

"A lion! and he did not devour you?"

"No, my father; on the contrary, he praised my comely looks, then offered to see me home, and came with me to the hamlet gate."

The Arab thought his child was mad.

"Impossible!" he cried.

"How impossible?"

"How am I to believe that a lion is capable of such an act of gallantry?"

"Shall I prove it to you?"

"Yes; but by what means?"

"If you go to the tent door, you will see him, either sitting where I left him, or returning to his home."

"Wait till I take down my gun."

"Why, am I not with you?" replied the girl, in her pride and conceit; and drawing her father by the *burnous* she led him to the tent door, but the lion was nowhere to be seen.

"Very well," said the father; "I see how it is, you have been dreaming."

"My father, I swear to you I see him still."

"How did he look?"

"He was about four feet high and seven feet long."

"Well?"

"With a beautiful mane."

"Well?"

"Great eyes, bright as the topaz."

"Well?"

"And teeth like ivory, only —"

"Only what?"

Aïcha lowered her voice: "Only he had a shocking bad breath."

She had hardly uttered these words before a fearful roar thundered from behind the tent, then another sounded about half a mile off, and then another from near the mountains, after which they heard nothing more. There had been

"A FEARFUL ROAR THUNDERED FROM THE MOUNTAINS."

hardly an instant's interval between the roars. It was then evident that the lion, desiring to know what the young girl might say of him, had made a circuit and come up behind the tent to listen, and had gone off in great mortification at finding out this imperfection, — so much the more dangerous because those who are infected by it never perceive it themselves. A month passed by and no more was seen of the lion; and the maiden had forgotten him, save when she told the story to her companions to while away the warm hours of noon.

One day she went again, as before, to cut her fagots, her hatchet in her hand. Drawing near the scene of her first adventures, she heard a heavy sigh, and on looking around saw the veritable lion, seated a few steps off, watching her movements.

"Good-morning, Aïcha," he said in a very dry tone.

"Good-morning, my lord," returned Aïcha in a trembling voice; for she had not forgotten her remark in regard to his fetid breath, nor the triple roar of indignation that had followed that impolitic disclosure.

"Good-morning. What can I do that will be agreeable to you?"

"You can do me a favor."

"What is it?"

"Come close to me."

The girl tremblingly obeyed, but wished herself in her father's tent again.

"Now I am by you."

"Very well; raise your hatchet and give me a blow on the head."

"But, my lord, thou dost not think — "

"On the contrary, I have thought much about it."

"But, seignior — "

"Strike!"

"But, my dear lord — "

"Strike, Aïcha, I pray you."

"Hard or softly?"

"As hard as you can."

"But I shall hurt you."

"What is that to you? Strike!"

"Do you want me to?"

"I do."

The girl hesitated no longer, but gave a blow with her hatchet between the eyes of the lion, that left a bloody mark where it fell.

"Thank you," said the lion; and in three bounds he disappeared in the wood.

Since that time, it is said, have the lions carried the deep vertical wrinkle between the eyes that appears so remarkable when they raise their eyebrows.

"Dear me!" said Aïcha, disappointed in her turn, "he is not going to see me home to-day;" and she returned alone.

The news of this second encounter soon spread through the village, and the wisest *talebs* laid their heads together to resolve its meaning. After much thought, and frequent reference to the Koran, they discovered the hidden meaning, and translated it as follows: "God is great, and the lion doeth what he wills."

A month passed by, and Aïcha was again in the woods, gathering fagots for the evening fire. At the moment she cut the first limb from a cedar-tree its dense branches parted, and the lion stepped out, with the same melancholy countenance as before; but a gleam burned in his great eyes, that seemed to menace what they turned upon. The maiden wanted to fly; but those great eyes nailed her to the earth, and she could not move. The lion stepped up to her with his royal mien, and her heart ceased to beat for very terror.

"Look at my forehead," said the terrible lover.

"But the seignior will recollect that it was he that ordered me to do it, and that I only obeyed," said the young girl, in a voice quivering with terror and anxiety.

"Yes, and I thank you for it; but it was not of that I was going to speak to you."

"What, then, is it the seignior desires?"

"Look at this wound on my forehead."

"I see it."

"Has it healed?"

"Perfectly; it is quite well."

"That proves, Aïcha, that the wounds that woman gives to the body are very different from the ones she gives to the spirit: the one heals in a month, the other, never."

This axiom was spoken in a voice that made the tassels on the pine-tree quiver in the air. A woman's shriek rang through the forest. The lion's love had gone to sleep forever, and his sensual appetite had awakened. Tongue may not speak of what followed. Prophet of God, defend us!

The next day, the father of Aïcha, with all the stout men of the *douar*, hunted the woods for the fairest maiden of the Zerazer. When they reached the place where lay the fagots, they found the white *haik*, a hatchet, and a scalp of long braided hair; but never since that time has man seen or heard aught of Aïcha.

A GLIMPSE OF THE GREAT DESERT SAHARA.

From the mountain range south of Batna you gain your first glimpse of this sand sea, — a vast plain, sweeping away and away. It is like the ocean, boundless, save for the horizon's brim; the image of the ocean, it is heaving, undulating, in billows of sand. It bears upon its bosom, like the ocean, isles and islets, — the oases, — which are also found grouped into archipelagoes, as this one of Zeban, of which the palm islands of Biskra are the most accessible to the tourist.

This vast plain, without limit, unsurveyed, is the Sahara. Its boundaries are undefined, therefore many dispute them. Hence it is that some writers claim that it begins at one place and others at another. But the truth is that it has no fixed boundaries, like the ocean. It is constantly encroaching upon the fertile land, sweeping up its sand-billows upon the foot-hills of the mountains, sending its sand-storms flying over the Tell and the Metidja, even to the Mediterranean. Storms and hurricanes sweep over this vast plain as over the ocean; its oases are the resorts of predatory Bedouins and caravans, even as the palm islands of the Pacific are lairs for pirates and havens of rest for storm-tossed fleets. Nothing in Nature, perhaps, can present so dreary an aspect as the plains of the Sahara, except the fire-scathed crater of a volcano; and nothing is so welcome to the traveller and the caravan as the green bulk of an oasis, — as welcome as an island of refuge to a storm-tossed sailor.

CHAPTER XIII.

FROM TRIPOLI TO EGYPT.

E will not ask you to penetrate the Sahara, for one acre of sand is very much like another; nothing is to be gained by joining a caravan and attempting to cross it. Leaving the oasis of Biskra, we made our way to the coast. You may now be able to reach it by rail, without the discomforts of a caravan journey; and there you may eat the dates of the desert, and study the fierce Bedouin in his native wilds. Life is not always easy in these oases, where the date palms lift their feathery fronds above rills and fountains. Sometimes the water that fertilizes the palm-grove lies at a great depth from the surface, and is painfully brought up through the wells by means of a very primitive apparatus. A great skin sewed together, opened wide at one end, is lowered and raised by means of ropes passing over pulleys. You hear their creaking night and day, as the men, women, children, and donkeys labor incessantly; for all the palms and fruit-trees and all the gardens demand water or they die, and the people dependent on them die. All the people of the oases live by agriculture, and about their only excitement is the arrival or departure of a caravan, or the occurrence of a *razzia*. The caravans come to buy dates, and bring in return wool, spices, and cotton. The women weave the wool into garments, which they use at home, and some they dye in bright colors and sell again to

the caravans. The people are busy all the morning and the afternoon, but at mid-day everybody sleeps, enjoying the siesta; in the evening they dance and sing, and listen to music from rude instruments. About midnight all go to sleep, nearly everybody in the open air, to be awakened in the morning by the muezzin's call to prayer. The *razzia* rarely happens to the oasis-dwellers, but to the shepherds of the plains, or the pastoral people on the skirts of the oases. The *razzia* is a wholesale robbery of sheep or cattle by a band of Arabs. Nearly all the Arabs are robbers, after a

REPELLING ARAB ROBBERS.

fashion, believing that other people's property is something that belongs to them if they can get it. So bands of robber Arabs prowl about the country watching for plunder, and when they discover a flock of sheep or herd of cattle negligently guarded, they swoop down upon it, drive off or kill the herdsmen, and hurry the herds away to their camps. Then the plundered people will organize a pursuit; perhaps a skirmish will result, men are slain, and the blood thus spilt will be a pretext for more quarrels and murders, sometimes lasting through generations. Thanks to the wise con-

THE CITADEL OF TRIPOLI.

trol of the French wherever they are in power, the poor shepherd and husbandman are secure in their flocks and gardens.

From a port of the coast we took passage in a sailing vessel for Tripoli, — that solitary city of the desert coast. It was not a journey that repaid our toil, for it does not differ much from other Arab cities whose glory has departed. It has a beautiful harbor, where once the pirates lay in wait for Christian fleets, and has a magnificent background of forest, composed of palms, oranges, figs,

DECATUR SAILING INTO THE HARBOR OF TRIPOLI

and olives. Many were the deeds of valor performed by the intrepid Decatur in this vicinity during the war between the United States and Tripoli. Many mosques and castles adorn the ruinous old city, and many of the streets are spanned by arches that prevent opposite houses from falling in. The Tripolitan oasis is one of the very few verdure-spots in this dreary desert. "It makes a singular contrast, this fertile region, lying between two plains of yellow sand,—an emerald necklace round a tawny throat. Here a garden, where plants grow with marvellous energy, and the foliage of the lemon-tree doubles the shadow of the palm; and behind the walls the absolute desolation of the parched desert, dunes of fine moving sand swept into waves and curves by the wind. Then one is tempted to repeat, with the old philosopher, 'Water is life;' for the presence or absence of water is the key to the mystery."

It was not our original intention to extend our explorations beyond North Africa proper, and hence Tripoli should have been our last destination, as we had now visited all the Barbary States — Morocco, Algiers, and Tunis — from Tangier to Tripoli. Here we had observed all we had come for,— the Arab as he now lives in the country he had subjugated a thousand years ago. It was put to vote whether we should keep on to Egypt, or then and there terminate our journeyings for the year, reserving the Land of the Pyramids for another time. We had another month at our disposal, so it was unanimously voted to put that month into Egypt, even though the season was too far advanced for us to take the boat-journey up the Nile. Taking a sailing vessel for Malta, we then made direct connection with the steamer for Alexandria.

Although we went to Alexandria merely as an Egyptian port whence we might reach Cairo and the Pyramids, yet we discovered much of interest in this city founded by Alexander the Great. For does it not date from a very early period,— from the year 332 B. C.,— and does it not command the mouth of the Nile and give access to Cairo and Suez? Nineteen hundred years ago, history tells us, it was taken by the Romans; and it was then the centre of philosophy, religion, and culture. Here was the great Alexandrian library, said to have contained at one time seven hundred thousand volumes of manuscripts. This library was burned by order of the Caliph Omar when Alexandria was captured by the fanatical Arabs in 640. You remember, of course, the decree of the ignorant despot who believed only in the God of the Prophet,

A VIEW OF TRIPOLI.

Mahomet, and reckoned all books other than the Koran as useless and superfluous: "If these writings agree with the Koran they are useless, and need not be preserved; if they do not they are pernicious, and ought to be destroyed." And destroyed they were, furnishing fuel, it is said, for six months to heat the baths of Alexandria. Over six hundred years later a similar destruction of valuable books was ordered by Cardinal Ximenes, in Spain, of Arabic manuscripts, as precious, in their way, as those of the famous Alexandrian. Alexandria, to-day, is a most cosmopolitan city, swarming with Arabs, Turks, Persians, Armenians, Copts, and Jews, besides French, Italians, English, etc., and even Americans. Your reception by the beggars and donkey-boys is most cordial, and you need not lack for company if you are not particular about the quality. The European quarter of the city has fine houses, squares, and promenades, and the city is fast recovering from the brutal bombardment it suffered from the English war-ships a few years ago. It was not modern Alexandria we were most interested in, nor modern Egypt. As the reader knows, we had come here to observe the influence of the Arabs upon Egypt, and to study Oriental architecture. This object could best be attained by a visit to Cairo, and thence we went, by train, with hardly a day's delay. In going from Alexandria to Cairo by rail we skirt Lake Mareotis, a very shallow lake, which in the dry season is little else than a vast swamp. But thousands, perhaps millions, of water-fowl are seen here, such as ducks of many species, pelicans, ibis, herons, and other denizens of the watery regions; and hence great sport is found here by the gunners.

The journey by rail takes from five to seven hours, and the distance is about one hundred and thirty miles. We cross the famous Delta of Egypt, a country fertile in cotton, sugar-cane, and grain lands, which are divided by canals, and their fertility kept up by irrigation. We were extremely interested in the operation of raising the water from the canals to the irrigating ditches. "The *shadorf* is the arrangement most in vogue. It consists of a long pole, made heavy at one end and resting on a pivot, at the other end a bucket, or large water-tight basket, which is lowered to the water and filled, and, as the heavy end of the pole goes down, turns out its contents into a little gutter, whence it is worked by the foot into the appointed channels. Sometimes this is superseded by the *sakish*, which is a water-mill of cogged wheels, turned by a buffalo or camel, each revolution of the wheel working up a series of earthen pitchers which empty themselves into a trough or pool. More primitive still is the practice, in frequent use, of raising the water without any mechanical contrivance. Two men stand in the stream or canal with a waterproof basket between them, which they swing as regularly as clockwork, and throw the water on to the bank, when another stands ready to divert it into its proper place. Not less interesting is it to watch the Egyptians ploughing with the primitive wooden plough."

At last the minarets of Cairo come to view, and the train, as it halts, is surrounded by a miserable lot of Arabs, all anxious to seize our luggage and make off with it. The Professor, who had previously had a taste of Oriental travel, instructed us to keep the wretches at bay while he made a bargain with one of them to take our effects to a certain hotel. Once settled in our hotel, where we had all the comforts of Europe at our disposal, we made excursions to the various parts of the city. We bargained with two bright-looking donkey-boys to furnish us their services and their beasts, and we are glad to put on record that they served us faithfully and well. There were many objects of interest in Cairo to be seen. We visited and made many purchases in the bazaars, saw the dancing dervishes and Joseph's Well, the mosques and palace of Gezeereh, the tombs, the walls and gates of the city, — for Cairo was a walled city, with seventy-one gates, — and the famous museum at Boulak. Outside the walls we were attracted by the obelisk of Heliopolis, the ruins of Memphis, old Cairo and the Nilometer, the petrified forest and the pyramids. Some of the bazaars are devoted to porcelain and works of glass, some to boots and shoes and embroidered leather, others to jewelry and precious stones. Joseph's Well is a curiosity of the citadel, a circular opening fifteen feet in diameter and two hundred and ninety feet deep, descending to the level of the Nile. A winding staircase leads to the bottom, where donkeys are at work raising water to the citadel by an endless chain. The citadel itself commands the town, and is worthy of admiration. It was the scene of the infamous slaughter of the Mamelukes in the year 1811.

"The Mamelukes," said the Professor, "were a class of soldiery who ruled Egypt for a very long period. They were originally foreigners, and were first introduced into Egypt, by one of the sultans, about the middle of the thirteenth century, and called Bahri Mamelukes (Arabic *memalik*, a slave), or Mamelukes of the river, from the island in the river Nile where they trained to arms. They were the Sultan's body-guard at first; at length, becoming strong, they murdered their master and placed one Eybek, their own commander, on the throne. In 1517, the Mamelukes were overcome by the Turks, and Egypt was divided into twenty-four provinces, each one under a Mameluke *bey*, or governor, but ruled over by a Turkish viceroy. They were then about twelve thousand in number, but still were essentially foreigners, obtaining even their wives from abroad, by purchase.

"It is not yet a hundred years since Napoleon Bonaparte encountered the Mamelukes, when he invaded Egypt, in 1798; and it was when on his march from Alexandria to Cairo. 'The whole plain was covered with Mamelukes,' says a historian, 'mounted on the finest Arabian horses, and armed with pistols, carbines, and blunderbusses of the best English make, their plumed turbans waving in the air, and their rich arms and equipments glittering in the sun.'

"Entertaining a high contempt for the French force, as consisting almost entirely of infantry, this splendid barbaric chivalry watched every opportunity for charging them, nor did a single straggler escape the unrelenting edge of their sabres. Their charge was almost as swift as the wind; and as their severe bits enabled them to halt or wheel their horses at full gallop, their retreat was as rapid as their advance. Even the practised veterans of Italy were at first embarrassed by this new mode of fighting, and lost many men, especially when fatigue caused any one to fall out of the ranks, in which case his fate became certain. But they were soon reconciled to fighting the Mamelukes when they discovered that each of these horsemen carried his entire fortune about him, sometimes amounting to great sums of gold. It was at that famous Battle of the Pyramids, July 21, 1798, that the Mamelukes received a severe rebuke to their pride. Seven thousand of them attacked the French, who slaughtered them most mercilessly; more than half their number were slain. Within a comparatively short time we have had news of equally desperate valor on the part of the wild Bedouins of the desert, meeting with quite as sanguinary defeat, as, for instance, the attack of the fanatical Arabs upon the English forces of the upper Nile only a few years ago, and their enormous losses. Again and again they charged upon the British troops, only to be mown down in heaps by the guns of their foes before they could get within striking distance.

"Well, the French troops of Napoleon's army were not so well equipped as the British of ninety years later, with their repeating arms and Gatling guns; but Arab bravery and fanaticism were as true as a century ago. Said Bonaparte: 'Could I have united the Mameluke horse to the French infantry, I would have reckoned myself master of the world!' But the world was comparatively small at that time, and no account was taken by Napoleon of this New World of ours, in which the United States were then girding themselves for destiny. The French were driven from Egypt, and the Mamelukes somewhat regained their power. But they fell out with the Turks and were brought to the verge of destruction in 1811; and it was in this citadel of Cairo that Mehemet-Ali consummated that act of fearful treachery by which nearly five hundred Mameluke chieftains were put to death. He somehow beguiled them into the citadel and then closed the gates and ordered his soldiers to shoot them down. In like manner, you will remember, the avaricious Alvarado, lieutenant of Cortez in Mexico, enticed the Aztec chiefs and nobles within the temple court where the Spanish army was quartered, and then put them all to death. Of the entrapped Mamelukes only one escaped the slaughter; this was a *bey*, who leaped his horse from the parapet — a fearful plunge — and made his escape uninjured, though his horse was killed. The Mamelukes were afterward massacred throughout Egypt, and a few years later were unknown.

"Cairo was long the home of the fierce Arabs who came from Arabia and overran Egypt and thence the north coast of Africa, which we have been describing. Here we find the great archetypes of the mosques and palaces we saw in Algiers, in Tangier, and Tlemcen. The great mosque of Mehemet-Ali, though not very old, has a vast cupola and a spacious court. From above its pavilion a very extensive view is obtained of Cairo and its surroundings, — the city itself, with its many minarets and domes, beyond it the green fields of the Delta, the tombs of the Mamelukes, and the obelisk of Heliopolis. It has been called one of the finest views in the world; and to give it added attractiveness, the great pyramids rise in their grandeur above the banks of Mother Nile."

DONKEY-BOYS.

The Historian called our attention to the fancied resemblance of the ruins in Yucatan and Mexico to some of the Egyptian structures. He spoke especially of an island on the coast of Yucatan called *Las Mugeres*.

It is about five miles long, and half a mile wide in its broadest part, and is composed entirely of coralline stone. An old historian describes it well, and the astonishment with which the Europeans regarded the temples and idols of stone found there, — the first of the kind ever looked upon by Spaniards in the New World. The island was called by them *Las Mugeres*, — "The Women's Island," because, says the old writer, "there were there towers of stone, with steps, and chapels covered with wood and straw, in which many idols, that *appeared to be females*, were arranged in very artificial order." The Spaniards marvelled to see edifices of stone, — that up to that time they had not seen in these islands, — and that the people there clothed themselves so richly and beautifully, because they had on tunics and mantles of white cotton and in colors, ornamented with feathers, and with gold and silver jewelry. . . . The Indians were seen in great numbers, and an action ensued in which fifteen Spaniards were wounded and seventeen Indians killed. Where this defeat was sustained, there were three houses made of stone and lime, which were oratories, with many idols of clay, having countenances of demons, of women, and of other horrid figures. And while they fought, the priest, Alonzo Gonzalez, took from the oratories boxes in which were idols of clay and wood, with ornaments, adornments, and diadems of gold. This same "Women's Island," then, was the first land trodden by Spanish adventurers on the coast of Yucatan. Besides a large native population, this island also boasted of a numerous floating population of pilgrims, who came yearly from the mainland to offer sacrifices at the shrine dedicated to the female idols. This shrine still stands to-day on the narrowest part of the promontory, washed by the waves; and recent explorers have found there some of the veritable incense-burners in which the pilgrims burned fragrant styrax and copal before the chief goddess. The shrine itself, or altar of the goddess, is found in the inner room of a stone tower, which was known as the holy of holies; and it was on this altar that the adventurers found the images and idols which were destroyed by their fanatical chaplain, who replaced them by an image of the Virgin Mary, and celebrated Mass. Silent and deserted stands the lonely tower to-day, — a solitary sentinel overlooking the little bay.

On the western shore of Yucatan is Campeche, discovered by the first explorer of this coast, Hernandez de Cordova, in 1517. He landed on the site of Campeche, and found an Indian city there, filled with temples of stone, containing hideous idols in the shape of serpents. The natives met him in troops, and without wasting words kindled a fire, telling him and his soldiers that if they were not off and away before those fires had gone out, their extermination would be only the work of a short space of time. And Cordova and his soldiers heeded this warning and went, nor stood upon the order of their going. It was in 1540 that the present city was founded by Don Francisco de Montejo, and its name is derived from two words in the Maya dialect: *cam*, a serpent, and *peche*, an insect called by the Spaniards *garrapata*.

CHAPTER XIV.

THE PYRAMIDS AND THE NILE.

"N, to the pyramids!" was our watch-cry as soon as the sights of Cairo had been made to yield their lessons of value. We were all unanimous on this point, that we wanted to see the pyramids, but from different reasons. The Doctor merely wanted to see in how short a time he could climb to the summit of the Great Pyramid, and he scorned the statement by a British tourist that it would make him tired. "Tired!" he echoed. "Tired! Pooh! Have n't I climbed higher than that? Have n't I been up to the top of Mount Washington, — climbed up all sides of it, and all sorts of ways, — up the old bridle-path from Crawford's Notch, and up the cliffs through Tuckerman's Ravine, and over the railroad track to the summit, and is n't that more than fifteen times as high as that old pile of stones and rocks?" Mere height, we told him, was of little consequence; the interest attaching to the pyramids resulted from their age, from their mysterious character, and from their being the greatest works of the greatest people who lived at the time of their erection. The Historian had looked forward to his visit to Egypt for several years, and so had the Professor. They both regretted that the time at their disposal was so short, and that they had not come more thoroughly prepared for a longer journey up the Nile. To them,

these relics of a dead and departed people were of the greatest importance, and they approached them with feelings bordering upon reverence and awe.

In America, in Mexico, and in Central America the Professor had

MAN'S WILLING SLAVE.

PYRAMIDS AND SPHINX.

visited and examined the ancient structures and pyramids. He had climbed the terraced sides of the great earth-pyramid of Cholula, where Quetzalcoatl, the god of the air, once had a temple, and had slept in the sculptured palaces of Yucatan. He had seen some of the largest mounds left by the Mound-builders, and had wandered among the pueblos and cliff-dwellings of Arizona and New Mexico. Thus it was with intense interest that he regarded the pyramids of Egypt, the greatest of their kind. Our impatience was hardly to be repressed, until we had halted at the base of the Great Pyramid. The journey thither consumed but an hour or two, as there was a good road all the way, and it was not long after leaving the Arab beggars of Cairo before we were engaged in conflict with their brother barbarians at the pyramids. They wanted us to climb at once, and at least forty pairs of dirty hands were extended to our assistance by forty ferocious Arabs. We refused all offers, however, till we had seen the Sheik of the Pyramid, the chief thief of this robber-band, and secured his assent and consent, by the payment of a small sum of money, — about a dollar for each member of our party. Of course *the* Great Pyramid was the one we climbed, in preference to the others. There are at least three large pyramids at Ghizeh, and several smaller ones, besides many tombs and (what has been called by some the greatest curiosity of all) the Sphinx.

The Great Pyramid, or the ancient sepulchre of Cheops, is 460 feet in height, has a base-line of 732 feet, and covers an area of 535,824 feet. Its height is twice that of Bunker Hill Monument, with twenty feet to spare. One might imagine that the pyramid was a solid mass; but about forty feet from the base-line, on the northern side, is an opening from which a vaulted gallery descends to a subterranean chamber nearly three hundred and fifty feet from the entrance. This chamber is about ninety feet below the base of the pyramid itself, is about 11 feet in height, 46 feet long, and 27 feet wide. An upward-leading passage, some sixty feet from the outer air, conducts toward the centre of the pyramid, and reaches at a distance of 125 feet, the so-called Great Gallery. Another, a horizontal passage 110 feet long, leads to the Queen's Chamber, 18 feet long and 20 feet high. The Great Gallery is 151 feet long, 7 feet wide, and 28 feet high, with a surface of polished stone, and leads upward to a vestibule which is said to have been obstructed by a portcullis of massive granite. The chief room in this pyramid is the King's Chamber, 34 feet in length, 17 feet broad, and 19 feet high, in which are the remains of an open sarcophagus of red granite. Higher yet are other rooms, but without any special feature of attraction.

About four thousand years ago (roughly computing), learned archæologists say, this chief pyramid was begun, the first of the Egyptian monuments of this character. The second Pyramid, supposed to have been built by Cephrenes, brother to Chaopa, has a base-line of 690 feet, and is 447 feet in height. The third pyramid has a base-line of 333 feet, and is but 203 feet in height.

But enough of statistics, of measurements, and speculations as to the origin and antiquity of the pyramids. As the works of men are measured they are vast, awe-inspiring; beside the works of the Creator they are as specks of sand compared with the walls of the Alps. Man comes here to wonder; he climbs painfully their broken sides, gazes at the monuments of the past about him, shakes his head solemnly, and departs, wondering at the mighty works of the departed Egyptians. Even so did we. With the assistance of two or three Arabs apiece, one on each side and another to push, we successfully scaled the Great Pyramid. Even the Doctor, who was so scornfully confident, did not disdain the assistance of two Arabs; and after he had reached the summit, and had seated himself to rest, he was heard to remark that even the cliffs above Tuckerman's Ravine were n't any harder to surmount. But even the Doctor confessed that the view from the

EGYPTIAN GARDEN AND TEMPLE.

summit more than repaid us for the great exertion. And it was not any more the scenes spread out around us than the mental pictures of the past these scenes evoked, that made our climbing of the pyramid memorable.

Four thousand years! A thousand years have rolled by since the interior of the pyramid was opened — forcibly opened — by the Caliph El Mainoon. Not far away, perhaps a quarter of a mile, crouched the Sphinx, the "Father of Immensity." Its body, mainly of the natural rock, is 140 feet in length, its paws are 50 feet in length, its massive head 30 feet from brow to chin. The Sphinx is said to be of greater antiquity than even the pyramids, to have existed long before the Great Pyramid was built. Listen to what the learned Kinglake says of it: —

"Upon ancient dynasties of Ethiopian and Egyptian kings; upon Greek and Roman, upon Arab and Ottoman conquerors; upon Napoleon, dreaming of an Eastern empire; upon battle and pestilence; upon the ceaseless misery of the Egyptian race; upon keen-eyed travellers; upon Herodotus yesterday and Warburton to-day, — upon all, and more, this unworldly Sphinx has watched and watched."

Not far away was old Cairo, opposite which is the island of Roda, where we may find the famed Nilometer, that invention of the ancients which marks the annual rise of the river Nile. Another ancient place is Heliopolis, where once stood the Temple of the Sun, and where to-day is an obelisk said to lead one farther back into antiquity than any other monolith in Egypt.

Standing upon the summit platform of the Great Pyramid, with so much of Egypt invitingly spread out before us, little wonder that we sent our gaze wistfully into the unknown regions of the farther Nile. We could not take the boat-journey up the Nile that we would have liked; but we could send our thoughts ahead, and in imagination sail the placid waters of this river of mysteries. During the winter months steamers make the journey as far as the Second Cataract of the Nile. Passing the pyramids, the Nilometer, and the site of ancient Memphis, — once the capital of Egypt, with its wonderful tombs and Colossi, — we may see other rock tombs, containing beautiful picturings, at Beni-Hassan, one hundred and seventy-one miles from Cairo. Far beyond, perhaps three hundred and fifty miles from Cairo, and six miles or so from the river-bank, are the ruins of Abydos, where the remains of two fine temples and an Acropolis attract thousands of visitors. But the most magnificent city of the past is Thebes, for the exploration of which the steamer stops at the river village of Luxor.

"The architecture of Egypt may be divided into three periods. The first is represented by the pyramids, dating from the time of the Memphian kings, and believed to be the oldest structures existing. The second period is the one which has bequeathed to the world the indestructible magnificence of the ruins of Karnak and Luxor, and is referable to the dynasties reigning at Thebes. The third has left behind it the temples of Hermonthis and Philæ, and represents the Ptolemaic rulers of Egypt. The great temple palace of Karnak is perhaps the noblest structure ever built by human hands. Its principal dimensions are 1200 feet in length by 360 in breadth, thus covering more than twice the area of St. Peter's at Rome. Its Hypostyle Hall alone is 340 feet long and 170 broad, — an area more extensive than that of Cologne Cathedral."

And here we find temples, tombs, sarcophagi, the larger structures ornamented with bas-reliefs and paintings. Here is the Rameseum, or the Memnonium, "without a rival in Egypt for elegant sculpture and architecture." It was built by Rameses II., the praises of whose greatness are inscribed on the walls. In front of the first court are two partly demolished pylons. One of these structures seems to stand by a curiosity of equilibrium. Both are adorned by sculptures representing battle-scenes in the campaigns of Rameses. In this court was once the most gigantic statue in Egypt, cut from the solid block of granite, and about fifty-four feet in height. The Colossi, both representing Amunoph III., once stood before the pylon of the temple of that monarch, and were nearly sixty feet high. One of these great statues was the famous "Vocal Memnon," so called from the sounds which issued from it when first reached in the morning by the rays of the sun.

The ruins of Luxor are equally celebrated; and here stands the companion obelisk to that one now to be seen in the Place de la Concorde, in Paris. Seven hundred and thirty miles from the mouth of the Nile is the town of Assouan, the ancient city of Syene, where tropical products are brought up from the distant Southland, such as gums and elephant ivory, and the people are strange and rare. The island of Elephantine lies opposite Assouan, sometimes called by its Arabic name, — Island of Flowers. Only three miles above Assouan is the First Cataract of the Nile, the passage of which may be made by *dahabeah*; but the steamer-voyage ends here, unless you wish to proceed in another by transfer. At the cataract, or the rapids, we meet with the Nubians, whose country, Nubia, lies to the south. Emerging into the river above the First Cataract, we see the islands of Philæ and Beghieh.

Philæ is called the Key of the Cataract; it has been successively held and defended by different peoples, but now lies in ruins, — a dead city in a desolate country. Here begins the Upper Nile, which may be navigated to the Second Cataract, over two hundred miles from this point. Egypt proper ends and Nubia begins here, and we are in the Biblical land of the Ethiopians. The climate in the winter season is mild and delightful, and boating on the Upper Nile a rich experience. Even here, so far from the fertile country of the Lower Nile, we find the architectural works of ancient man. At Ipsambool is the Great Temple, which one writer calls "the most impressive of the monuments of Egyptian grandeur." The Second Cataract has long been the returning-point of ordinary tourists. Claiming to be nothing more than travellers of average ambition with a taste for exploration, though without the time for unlimited adventure, we will not seek to penetrate farther. Beyond, far beyond, is the real, the mysterious Dark Continent, — the Africa of Bruce and Baker, Livingstone and Stanley. We cannot hope to even follow in their footsteps, — at least, not now, — so we will withdraw our thoughts from the scenes of their adventures. Stanley's province lies south of the Equator, where he has won immortal fame. Quite near the equatorial line are the great Murchison Falls, discovered by Sir Samuel Baker in 1862. We would gladly extend our journey so far; but even this Nile journey is only ours in imagination. Having remained late in Algiers, — till the winter was past, — we came to Egypt too late for extended travel. From the pyramid-top we had projected our vision into the region of the Upper Nile. Here, too, we say farewell. If we have not given you new information or ideas, it is not because we have not desired to be of service to you. What says the great philosopher? "A man's nature runs either to herbs or weeds; therefore let him seasonably water the one and destroy the other." Think upon grand things, project noble schemes and studies that shall elevate; reach up and beyond, rather than down and near, is the closing advice of the members of this "Knockabout Club."

www.ingramcontent.com/pod-product-compliance
Lightning Source LLC
Chambersburg PA
CBHW021810230426
43669CB00008B/695